Singing Meditation

Singing Meditation

Together in Sound and Silence

Ruthie Rosauer and Liz Hill

Boston
Skinner House Books

Printed in the United States

Cover design by Kathryn Sky-Peck
Text design by Suzanne Morgan
Cover art "A Thousand Beautiful Things," © 2004 Cindy Kane,
www.cindykane.com

ISBN 1-55896-557-2
978-1-55896-557-7

13 12 11 10
6 5 4 3 2 1

Library of Congress Cataloging-in-Publication Data

Rosauer, Ruthie.
  Singing meditation : together in sound and silence / Ruthie Rosauer and Liz Hill.
    p. cm.
  ISBN-13: 978-1-55896-557-7 (alk. paper)
  ISBN-10: 1-55896-557-2 (alk. paper)
  1. Singing—Religious aspects. 2. Meditation. I. Hill, Liz, 1955- II. Title.
  ML2900.R67 2009
  203'.8—dc22
                            2009021334

We gratefully acknowledge permission to reprint the following copyrighted materials: "Mold clay into a vessel…" from Lao Tzu, *Tao Te Ching* Verse 11, translated by Hua-Ching Ni, in *The Complete Works of Lao Tzu* (Santa Monica, CA, Seven Star Communications, 1995), 18, reprinted with permission from Seven Star Communications, 800/772-0222, www.taostar.com; "Namaste," words and music by Nickomo Clarke, from *Here Right Now* songbook and CD, available at www.nickomoandrasullah.com, used by permission; "Dhanyavad" by Henry Marshall (www.inpeacenet.com), from *Mantras: A Musical Path to Peace*, copyrighted and used by permission; "Fill Your Cup," music by Allaudin Ottinger, from *In the Everywhere and Always*, copyrighted and used by permission; "May There Be Peace," words and music by Nickomo Clarke, from *Singing with the Angels* songbook and CD, available at www.nickomoandrasullah.com, used by permission; "Mother I Feel You," words and music by Windsong Dianne Martin © 1996, used by permission; "Joy," by Helen Gierke, © 2009, used by permission.

This book is dedicated to Tim and Karen Hirsch. It would never have been written without their encouragement, enthusiasm, and beautiful voices from the very beginning.

A song is a thing of joy; more profoundly, it is a thing of love.

—St. Augustine

Contents

Introduction

"Fill your cup, drink it up! A fish in the water's not thirsty!" These lines, penned by the Indian mystic and poet Kabir several centuries ago, offer a perfect entrée into the world of singing meditation. His words celebrate the way we live our lives, swimming in an ocean of divine love; all we need do is open ourselves to its presence and drink it in.

The goal of singing meditation is to create a time and space for our souls to explore their vast potential for spiritual joy. We can live such that our lives flow on in waves of delight and contentment. All too often, we forget this possibility, as we wade through the channels carved by our busy lives. Our spirits grow parched and we forget to drink, focusing instead on the sun burning our faces and the other pesky fish devouring tasty morsels before we can. We thirst. We forget to live mindfully in this universe of unending abundance.

Singing meditation opens us to this possibility by combining two time-honored spiritual practices: singing out to the divine mystery and sitting silently to listen for a response. Its beauty and power lie in the alternation and juxtaposition of these two disciplines. Communal song carries us deeply into the silence of our authentic selves. Regardless of our spiritual backgrounds, this interfaith experience can unite us in a community of voices and hearts, and help us recover the lost voices of our souls.

The singing part of the practice includes toning, chanting, singing in rounds, and harmony. The repertoire of short, simple songs is drawn from a variety of spiritual paths, and even novice singers can quickly learn most of them. A facilitator leads the sessions, selecting and teaching the songs. Each session begins in a learning mode, the facilitator playing the melody line or singing alone, repeating the song until others feel confident enough to join in.

Singing with eyes closed, we savor the web of musical vibrations woven through and around us. We become attuned to the subtle changes of other singers as the vocalizing grows louder, builds in volume, then ebbs softly to a slower pace. We stop worrying about other people's opinions. We simply sink into the lagoon of sound and relax. The blending of voices releases our busy minds and directs our attention inward, framing the silence that follows each song.

With no deliberate cue, songs naturally dissolve into silence, and we sit quietly for two to five minutes. The facilitator does not direct these silent periods. We might choose to use the intervals for meditation, prayer, or contemplation. The words of the song may echo through our minds as the sound continues to reverberate through the silence. Together we share the sacred space we have created between sound and silence. Chinese philosopher Lao Tzu poetically describes this empty silence:

Thirty spokes together make a wheel for a cart.
It is the empty space in the center which enables it
    to be used.
Mold clay into a vessel;
it is the emptiness within that creates the usefulness of
    the vessel.
Cut out the doors and windows in a house;
it is the empty space inside that creates the usefulness
    of the house.
Thus, what we have may be something substantial,
But its usefulness lies in the unoccupied, empty space.

The substance of your body is enlivened
By maintaining the part of you that is unoccupied.

When the facilitator signals the end of the silent period, we focus our attention back to the group again, and the facilitator leads us into the next song. We let our voices soar once again. Novice singers may be delightfully surprised to find themselves part of a group singing so easily in a round or in harmony. As that song fades, we again hold silence. We might take a few moments to stare into a candle's flame or contemplate the words of the song. Or we might close our eyes and surrender to interior silence and tranquility, trusting in the divine mystery.

In this way, a session layers sensation upon sensation. As we visit and revisit melody, harmony, silence, chant, and silence again, we create a pastiche of depth and complexity. Contentment segues into joy, which then dissolves into a silence brightened by clarity. Unfamiliar songs insinuate their patterns into our minds and become guiding stars to our constellation of voices.

The practice aims to disconnect the mind from the grasp of its perpetual routine, worries, grievances, timetables, and fears. Enchanted by sound and vibration, the mind releases its dominion of the self. In the quiet, the heart holds sway. Freed from the mind's heavy yoke, it leaps into the current of joy, cavorting in the melody, then rests quietly where song laps gently against silence, again and again. We are free to seek our soul's source, trusting in the universe to lead us where we can once again fill our cup. A fish in the water's not thirsty!

This book introduces singing meditation to those who want to experience or facilitate the practice. The last two chapters offer advice specifically for those who would like to start and lead a group. Singing meditation is designed to be interfaith. The only prerequisite for attending is a desire to join others in sending your voice toward the heavens. Even if you think you can't carry a tune, you are welcome as a full participant. We invite you to explore this spiritual practice with a song based on the words of Rumi:

Come, come, whoever you are
Wanderer, worshiper, lover of leaving
Ours is no caravan of despair. Come, yet again come.

Everyone Is Invited

Come, come, whoever you are. As enticing as the invitation sounds, some might still wonder if their voices would be welcome at a singing meditation session. The answer is a resounding yes!

The co-authors of this book traveled very different paths to singing. Ruthie sang almost before she could talk, but Liz decided early on that she couldn't sing. Now, however, we both use singing meditation as a bridge to the divine. In this chapter, we each tell our own story in our own words. We also include information about the power of singing in community—a community we invite you to join.

Our society has become a nation of musical spectators rather than singers and players. Some people, listening to their own internal critics, have shut down their singing altogether. Others have succumbed to the harsh words of a sibling or a grammar school teacher. Many people think that if their voices don't measure up to an electronic, digitally remixed, mastered perfection, they don't have the right to sing. We have empowered a tiny cadre of professional musicians to make music for us, and in turn silenced our own voices. Singing meditation helps people reclaim their singing voices by encouraging singers of all abilities to dive into the river of sound and trust in the community of voices for support.

Americans spend nearly half their total food budget on food prepared by others in restaurants, but that doesn't stop most peo-

ple from cooking in their own homes. Although we hire professional photographers for weddings, we don't stop taking pictures
ourselves. Let singing be another activity we enjoy as amateurs.

Ruthie: A Singer's Story

I grew up in a family that regularly attended a fundamentalist Christian church. On Sunday mornings, we went to Sunday school followed by church; on Sunday evenings, we went to church again and
stayed for "afterglow." On Wednesday evenings, we attended prayer
meeting. Youth group met on Saturday nights. Music was the part
I loved best about attending church services. During the singing,
my heart was uplifted, I felt close to God, and my entire being felt
suffused with grace and joy. Our church encouraged people to start
singing any time the spirit moved them. Music was not confined
to three hymns and the doxology listed in the church bulletin but
sometimes burst forth spontaneously as a joyful event, connecting
our voices in community while we poured our souls out to the Lord.

I left that church in 1969 at the age of sixteen, although I
continued to search for a meaningful connection with the divine
in a variety of religious traditions. I heard a lot of beautiful music
in the process but deeply missed the heartfelt singing of my childhood church. Sadly, no substitute activity made me feel as uplifted
and joyful as gospel singing. By rejecting the church's doctrine, I
feared I had lost forever the powerful feelings the music engendered. I lived thirty years without the joy of singing in community.
Not until I spent time with the Findhorn Community, a New Age
intentional community in Scotland, did I begin to find my way
back to sacred music.

Spiritual singing took place at Findhorn every morning before
the workday. Although the community advocates no specific spiritual path, at that time their music meditation repertoire consisted
only of Christian music written or collected by a monastic community in Taizé, France. (For more about Taizé, see page 31.) It
emphasized the blending of voices and moments of quiet between

songs. Although we sang in rounds and harmonies, we did not rehearse. No audience was present, anticipated, or invited. We experienced singing as meditation in its own right.

The repetition of melodic lines, especially when sung with others, quieted both my soul and mind. At first I concentrated on getting the notes and words right, afraid of making a mistake. I didn't want to offend anyone by singing too loudly. I also worried that I might be off pitch and annoy others. This block is common—the fear of outside criticism or disapproval inhibits our innate joy in singing. For many, the fear of judgment is so strong that they have stopped singing entirely.

As my familiarity with the music grew, I found I could let go of the printed words. I was then released into the music—and through the music into another sphere. I connected to something larger than myself. I stopped worrying about what was coming out of my mouth and felt the transcendence of being within the sound itself. I realized that I had glimpsed a way to reclaim the spiritual power of song without worrying about religious doctrine or criticism of my vocal expression.

After Findhorn, I experimented with ways to tap into this wellspring of joyful singing. I sang alone at home with the CDs I had purchased at the Taizé and Findhorn communities, before an altar I had created with stones and candles. But singing alone only underscored my loneliness. Singing formally in choral groups did not fulfill my yearning for a musical community either. I wanted my soul to soar again, secure in the sound of voices mingling with my own. I needed to sing with others but without the constraints of perfect execution.

In May 2004, I offered the first singing meditation session in Eau Claire, Wisconsin. I hoped to create a hybrid spiritual practice—combining the joy of singing, the energy of community, and the power of silence—to provide transformation without undue direction.

Singing meditation disconnects me from this world and connects me with my spiritual core. It nourishes my soul. Best of all, I can feel my spirit swelling and rising with joy as it did so long ago in the church of my youth. I have offered this practice monthly in Eau Claire ever since.

Liz: A Former Nonsinger's Story

Music saturated my childhood home. To be more accurate, it assaulted, overwhelmed, and tormented me. Music was my father's passion, in the truest sense of the word's etymology, from the Latin *pati*, "to suffer or endure." That's how music felt in my house. Whenever my father was home, his hi-fi speakers relentlessly blasted opera, classical, or sacred music, often to the accompaniment of a lecture explaining the work or its composer. I found music immensely intimidating.

I understand that some might consider my childhood exposure to the classics a wonderful gift. And it might have been, had we been enticed to the table by the lure of promising aromas; had we been allowed a sample now and again, to test and develop our taste buds; had we been encouraged to process our reactions and express our preference for one flavor over another. But in my house, music was not to be explored or savored—we were told to sit down and listen, and we'd better learn to like it.

As a result, my siblings and I developed passions of our own that were not musical. I loved to write and lost myself in a world of books and poems and stories. Sadly, though, I really loved music. My mother recalls that as a young child, I spent hours beside a small record player, singing along with my little yellow records. But the joy of those simple songs fell by the wayside as I learned about "real" music from my father. My sister studied the violin for a while, and at some point I was offered music lessons, but I refused. Frankly, learning to play looked hard and sounded worse. More important, I knew I could never meet my father's expectations if I stepped into his territory. Why open myself to criticism? Why call attention to my lack of talent? I could pursue reading and writing stories quietly on my own. Making my own music would be too public a humiliation to risk.

In junior high, I auditioned for a choral group to socialize. Most of my friends made the cut, but I didn't, confirming what I had already suspected: I was not a musician or a singer, and I never would be. Henceforth, I confined my singing to the shower, the privacy of my bedroom, and the car. I remained an avid fan of folk and pop music, but I left singing to the singers. My gift was writing—that was the medium where my voice would be heard.

I met Ruthie Rosauer in 1989. She sang well and played several instruments. Although we both enjoyed music, I held fast to my decision and let her do the singing. As our friendship grew, we discovered that we were compatible travelers. On our first trip to Europe, as we strolled beneath the blue skies of Edinburgh, Scotland, Ruthie launched into "Bonnie Banks o' Loch Lomond." Naturally, she expected me to join with enthusiasm. Aside from the fact that my vocal chords were atrophied, I was mortified at the very thought of anyone singing in public, especially when the singer was walking beside me.

It would be hard to find two more opposing approaches to singing, but somehow our friendship survived. Visiting Ruthie at the Findhorn Community in Scotland a few years later, I had my first encounter with Taizé singing. Ruthie was so jazzed about this practice that I felt duty-bound to try it. I warbled along softly, partly because the music was unfamiliar, but mostly because the sound of my own voice rang foreign in my ears. The music was beautiful, and I enjoyed being part of the group, certain that my voice contributed very little to the creation of its heavenly sound.

When I lived in Denver, I occasionally attended Dances of Universal Peace, a spiritual practice using song and dance to celebrate the name of God. I enjoyed singing the short, simple songs that accompanied the dances (*sotto voce*, of course). I realized that singing made me feel good.

In 1999, I joined a church whose music director encouraged everyone to sing. Over time, I grew less timid about singing out on Sundays as part of the congregation, hoping I wasn't ruining anyone else's experience. No one complained. In fact, someone suggested

I join the choir. Of course, I didn't take them seriously. I don't read music, and I certainly didn't sing well enough for a choir.

I now realize that silencing my singing voice was a way of avoiding the possibility of making mistakes. Mistakes imply failure, and failure could be disastrous. Unfortunately, my singing was not the only victim of this philosophy. Making my writing public also feels risky, and although I have published several books and stories, I have also allowed myself to be distracted, dissuaded, and discouraged by rejection.

In 2004, Ruthie began to lead singing meditation in Wisconsin. We still lived in different states, so I could not attend, but her passion to follow her heart's call inspired me. At about that time, my husband also decided to launch a dramatic career change. While in the throes of all the churning, something began to nudge my soul awake. I revived my passion for writing, completing a novel I'd started years before. I recalled my childhood longings and decided to try them again. I danced and drummed. Poetry sprang from my pen without warning, and I suddenly found myself singing as my morning tea steeped, as I walked my dog in the gray winter fog, as I chopped vegetables for a hearty pot of soup.

My biggest surprise came on a vision quest, when I spent three days and nights alone in the woods on a pristine lake in Vermont. During a vision quest, you strive to become one with nature, and in the process your true self is invited to emerge. Naturally, I began my quest with attention to personal safety, but in less than an hour, I'd set up my shelter and arranged my limited equipment. After that it was just the loons, the trees, the clouds, my water jugs, and me. Page after page of scribble filled my journal on the first day, and as the sun disappeared behind the sacred mountain, lo and behold, I began to sing.

I sang for three days. Stretched out like a lizard on a rock, I sang songs I had learned in school, like "The Erie Canal" and "Old Man River." I lulled myself to sleep with hymns and Taizé songs I'd learned from Ruthie. When the animals rustled in the woods at midnight, I serenaded them with gospel songs and politely asked them to move along. All of my songs were duets, grown-up Liz alongside that little girl beside the record player. My truest voice, along with my soul, was well on the road to recovery.

When I moved to St. Paul, I finally had a chance to experience singing meditation. I was nervous, of course. This practice was my friend's passion! Could I possibly share her enthusiasm? But we had discussed writing this book, and we both knew that I had to understand what singing meditation felt like.

At my first session, Ruthie reassured the participants that only presence and intention mattered, not the quality of our voices. We began with simple songs and really had fun. But when we started a more complex song, I couldn't seem to distinguish the melody line from the harmony lines. Frustrated and confused, I felt my old childhood panic creep back and settle in. *Ah*, it whispered, *here we are again. You know you can't sing. It's obvious. Everyone's listening. They can tell. Why are you here? Who do you think you are?*

I plunged forward, refusing to give in. When I sang, no one laughed or grimaced. Our singing harmony sounded startlingly wondrous. After a few repetitions, my voice failed once again, not in terror or frustration but in awe. I was moved to tears. Am I part of this? Can I possibly be hitting the right notes while someone beside me sings different notes? This was not the same as listening to a choir. My voice blended with this group, became part of its sound. Quickly, I joined in again so I wouldn't miss a single note of my harmonic debut.

To my surprise, the challenging song ended far too quickly, and we moved on to another easier song. My confidence swelled as part of this inclusive community. The weaker singers like me keyed off the stronger singers, and the group as a whole encouraged me to sing out. After a few tries, even the tricky songs were familiar enough to manage. No one seemed to care which individual was responsible for our joyous noise. Gradually, a sense of peace descended during the singing and deepened during the silence.

I admit that singing meditation did not move me to a place of transcendence on the first try. I had too much to think about to really relax into the music or the meditation. But since my second try, I have many times experienced moments when the sound surrounded and suffused me. And the silence brings a powerful contrast, an invitation to go deeper. Singing meditation helps me approach God in a new way, with both joy and reverence.

Most likely, if you were attracted to this book, you are already a singer or musician. You probably don't need to be convinced to try singing meditation. But I hope it's clear from my story how much someone else might need *you*. Each time Ruthie leads a new group, she hears stories like mine: "I thought I couldn't sing" or "I haven't sung in years" or "I forgot how much fun it was to sing." A session can open a world of joy for someone to whom the door closed long ago.

The Spirit of Community

We've all experienced a sense of wonder and magic when a great choir performs sacred music. Sometimes the sound feels as comfortable as a soft blanket on a cold night. At other times, its power and majesty roll over us like a huge wave, knocking us to our knees. The musical experience touches us deeply in a mysterious way, awakening our emotions.

The effect is even greater when we participate in singing together. Joined in song, our emotions are not merely stirred; they merge and dissolve with the emotions of others, deepening our human connection. Our voices create a net of sound that binds us tightly together. When we gather to sing sacred songs, the song and the act of singing together strengthen our spiritual community by bolstering our sense of fellowship.

The word *spirit* is derived from the Latin *spirare*, "to breathe." The act of singing moves our breath, the essence of our spirit, from our deepest core out into the atmosphere. When we sing together in singing meditation, the benefits are reciprocal: The act of singing strengthens the community, and the group's camaraderie enhances the beauty and power of the songs.

Singing in community produces a tangible power that doesn't exist when we sing alone. As an experiment, sing a song alone, then sing with recorded music, then sing the same song in the presence of others who are singing the same song. Notice which of these forms affects you most powerfully.

Singing in community increases the effect music has on us. Katy Taylor, a professional singer, compares her spiritual connection when singing with a group to singing solo: "Group singing is a different kind of connection. In a group, it is not about any one single voice being heard. We are together creating something. It is much more about interaction, an energy and blending between us, and hopefully that leads to movement toward the divine."

Performing alone demonstrates a higher level of proficiency in some activities. Flying an airplane solo or mounting a solo art exhibition require a certain level of mastery. Only the best musicians and singers are awarded these opportunities.

However, mastery is not the point of singing meditation. Its purpose is to move the soul towards—or even into—the divine impulse. A single carbon atom transmutes into an entirely different substance—a protein, an alcohol, maybe an acid—when joined and energized with other atoms. Similarly, an individual voice transmutes into something new and wondrous when joined with others in heartfelt song or chant. Each voice singing in community becomes part of a vibrational field or structure that did not exist before.

Many world religions recognize the power of community worship and have institutionalized it in their practices. Praying alone is permissible in Judaism, but many prayers are written in the first-person plural—"us" and "we," rather than "me" and "I." Some prayers acknowledge the importance of souls linking with other souls when approaching the divine presence.

Theravada Buddhists recommend group chanting, believing that it develops the collective mind. Proponents of Hindu *bhajan*, which can only be practiced in a group setting, say that group chanting reduces stress, resulting in mental relaxation and a feeling of camaraderie. When asked whether group or individual meditation is better, one teacher of *preksha* meditation said that group meditation makes the vibrations of the life force stronger because each individual's power becomes available to the others.

Tim and Karen, who have attended singing meditation sessions for several years, agree that singing in a group is a richer experience. They told us, "Singing alone can be meditative, prayerful, healing, expressive, and/or joyful. But singing with a group from time to time is essential—part of our definition of singing. It is a fuller spiritual experience, more playful and fun, more memorable."

People who sing in harmony with others, reaching out in sensitivity and trust to the group energy, attest to its intensity, which remains even as the last musical tone fades away.

The Singing Meditation Experience

Participating in a religious ritual for the first time can be daunting. Unfamiliarity with other religions makes some people anxious. For example, some people not raised in the Catholic faith feel confused about when to sit, stand, or kneel during Mass. Their anxiety makes it difficult to completely relax and enjoy the experience.

Singing meditation draws music from a variety of religious traditions. The sessions are not a performance or a rehearsal for a performance—they provide a spiritual, emotional, and physical experience on their own. The practice aims to create a worship experience accessible to all without the barriers of creed, language, or memorized words and rituals. No musical background or specific religious affiliation is required. Although a session may include inspirational quotes or readings, there are no sermons or liturgical readings.

Sessions may be offered in a series or on an occasional basis. Participants can drop in to an individual session without feeling obligated to continue attending. Although sessions can vary in length, an hour is typical. Sessions at weekend retreats may last two hours. The setting is usually informal, with chairs or pillows arranged in a circle or semicircle. A table or altar, adorned with candles, scarves, or flowers, may serve as a focal point in the center of the circle.

The facilitator gives verbal instructions at the beginning of the session and throughout. Participants need only sing when the group is singing and be silent when the group is silent.

Toning

Sessions often begin with toning—vocalizing long, sustained sounds, usually open vowel sounds or single syllables. Toning warms up the vocal cords and helps shy singers feel less concerned about their musical ability or voice quality. Everyone can relax and tone. A person can tone alone, but those who have tried both individual and group toning report that group toning is much more powerful; the toning vibrations are sustained even when individual toners must stop for breath. Group toning produces a sound that can be haunting, even eerie, because the intensity and pitch are unpredictable. At other times, the sound is better described as a peaceful wave of harmony rolling through the group, as toners adjust their pitches in response to what they hear and feel.

You can tone while sitting or standing. Keep the spine as straight as possible to allow the energy to flow freely in the body. Imagine your head suspended from above by a fine cord, your body hanging naturally below. Close the eyes and relax the jaw enough that the teeth are slightly parted. Relax the body so it can sway with the toning. Use a gentle voice—don't strain. Focus your energy and intent. Breathe in deeply and expand your lower abdomen as you inhale. The resulting sound should be mindful, not loud or even necessarily pretty. Repeat each tone (both pitch and vowel sound) many times.

In singing meditation we sometimes do a toning exercise that involves breaking into pairs, each partner taking turns toning toward the other's back for several minutes. One person who received this toning described the sound "O" as feeling like a soft shawl draped around her shoulders. Her body began to relax until she actually started to feel shaky, as if she needed to lie down. However, when she took her turn as the toner, this normally shy singer noticed a new calmness. While she typically would have stressed about whether she was doing it "right," she found herself able to focus better on toning and enjoy the experience.

People describe the toning in singing meditation sessions as grounding, healing, and affirming, and as a "pure" experience. Some participants find toning more mindless than singing, allowing them to go deeper into their subconscious. Proponents believe it can alter the body's cellular structures, activate energy centers, induce emotional release, and stimulate the body's innate healing power. Toning is said to restore and realign the vibrational pattern of the body so that each organ can attain its healthiest frequency.

Silence is particularly acute after a toning session. The surrounding air feels renewed, as if washed clean by sound, granting us a fresh start.

Singing

The most popular kinds of songs in singing meditation are chants, rounds, songs in harmony, and call-and-repeat songs. (These are explained more fully in the Glossary, on page 87.) The facilitator always demonstrates a song before inviting the rest of the group to join in. Knowing how to read music is not required, and singers of all levels may participate. Everyone learns at his or her own pace. Some participants may need to attend a few sessions before they reach the stage of carefree, heartfelt singing.

Tess had attended a few sessions over the course of a year. One day she sought Ruthie out, her face beaming with joy. She said, "This is the first time I felt like I really *knew* the songs we were singing. I didn't have to read the words. I just sang and sang and sang. I can't believe the difference!" Through singing meditation, Tess found that she could tap into her inner joy and wisdom as the music became more familiar to her.

Participants may just listen until they feel confident enough to join in. They should not, however, interrupt the group singing to ask the leader to repeat a particular part of the song, as one might do in a choir practice. After a song has ended, it is important to hold the silence. A sneeze or cough is sometimes unavoidable, but people should refrain from speaking, even to praise the quality of the singing or express feelings of joy or contentment.

The Words

People sometimes find song lyrics an obstacle. This problem stems from one of two sources: They do not believe in the literal meaning of the words being sung and feel dishonest singing them, or they are concerned about correct pronunciation.

The Taizé song "Jesus Remember Me" might cause discomfort for non-Christians, because it calls on a religious figure they do not believe in to remember them in heaven. Since singing meditation was deliberately created to be interfaith, it regularly uses songs that include names for Krishna, Allah, and other deities. But singing meditation does not require participants to sing lyrics that cause them discomfort. If these specific names for God become a stumbling block, singers simply substitute any open vowel sound or just hum instead.

Participants sometimes worry about correct pronunciation, particularly when singing songs in foreign languages, but in most cases, they need not fret. A minister friend recalls a Sufi class he took in seminary. Each class began with the traditional *salat*, with prayers said in Arabic. The non-Muslim American students had problems pronouncing and remembering the Arabic words. The professor reassured them by explaining the Muslim belief that angels watch over the faithful and listen to the recitation of the Koran. "Do not worry if you mispronounce the words," the teacher explained. "If you pray sincerely, the angels will carry the correct words to Allah." Some singing meditation songs are printed in more than one language, so participants can sing in the language they find most comfortable.

In some traditions, correct pronunciation *is* important. For example, the ancient Sanskrit mantras from India are believed to be mystical formulas capable of activating specific energies. They are composed of a series of sounds; some are actual words with specific meanings and others are meaningless syllables. Chanting these mantras has a vibrational effect on the physical body, whether or not the words are understood. The key to chanting these mantras is pronouncing them correctly.

Some teachers agree that the pronunciation of the words in a prayer is as important as the words themselves. David Cooper, author of *Silence, Simplicity and Solitude*, writes, "The content of a prayer and the intention behind it are only part of the necessary components; the actual sounding of the words and their proper enunciation is also a major ingredient." Cooper also believes that prayers should be recited in their native tongue to fully experience the power and melody of the words.

In singing meditation, the facilitator will explain to the group whether the exact text or pronunciation is critical.

The Silence

Silence has traditionally been used in spiritual practices, including prayer, contemplation, and meditation. (See "Silence and Spirituality" for more information.) However, those participants new to keeping silence in the presence of others may find their minds too filled with wonder (or worry) to become still easily. Counting breaths, as some Buddhists do, may help. Breathe in deeply, hold the breath, and count silently, "one." Then exhale. Repeat until ten breaths have been counted. Repeat again. If you are not used to meditation practice, you may be surprised how difficult it is to get to ten.

Alternatively, choose one word or phrase—perhaps taken from a song used in singing meditation—to focus the attention during the silent period. Don't approach the word intellectually or consider its etymology; just be receptive to sensory impressions that arise in conjunction with the word or phrase.

Silence can be an acquired taste. Participants who find it uncomfortable at first might consider this analogy: Imagine enjoying a ripe, juicy plum, and then wiping your mouth with the back of your hand or perhaps washing the juice from your face with cool, clear water—but also imagine that the essence of the plum remains. In this way, the plum's taste and feel lingers in its absence. Likewise, the vibrations that emanate from each individual during the singing linger during the silence. Singing meditation provides repeated opportunities to relish the lingering vibrations and savor the music pulsating in the silence.

Silent intervals generally last from two to five minutes. At the end of the interval, the facilitator rings a bell or strikes a gong. Silence continues for a few moments to allow for a gentle, gradual return of presence before the next song begins.

Participants soon become used to the alternating pattern of song and silence, and enjoy the interplay of the two sensations across their souls. Day and night. Light and dark. Summer and winter. Yin and yang. Song and silence. The contrast of differing elements deepens our awareness and appreciation of each.

Participants should take time to consider their reasons for attending singing meditation. If it is to satisfy their curiosity about how the practice will make them feel—excellent! If they hope the singing will quiet the mind, enabling them to pray, contemplate, or tap into an inner core of divine wisdom, these are also good reasons. However, if they are seeking vocal coaching or a chance to impress others with their vocal range, this practice will not be a good fit. It is also not intended for people desiring a homily or a sermon. A session may include a few inspirational readings or poems, but otherwise, the facilitator provides no formal spiritual direction. Participants who believe they have a good voice must leave their ego at the door. Judging the quality of vocal output during and after each song will get in the way of letting go and floating into the community voice created during singing meditation.

Patty, a singing meditation participant, has used her beautifully clear soprano voice in choruses, choirs, and informal groups for several decades. When describing the difference between singing in a group just for fun and the spiritual aspects of singing meditation, she cites the intention of the participants. For her, this spiritual practice provides "a sense of being totally absorbed in the sound. The sound is within you and surrounding you, and you're responding to that sound. It's a combination of being very tuned in to your own experience, following where it leads you, while at the same time being very tuned in to the sense of the group. Whatever it is, I find it very freeing and uplifting."

Participants should try to arrive at a session with an open heart and mind. Remember that others in attendance are also seekers. Be compassionate and respectful. Try not to distract them from their own path and to limit judgment of them. With these intentions, everyone can find joy in a singing meditation session.

Sacred Music Traditions

Songs that work well in singing meditation fill many of the traditional roles of sacred music. Each, however, must be capable of awakening that elusive quality we identify only as "spirit" in order to be part of the singing meditation repertoire. Today, songs that are simple to learn and that, by melody or vibration alone, touch our spirits and "fill our cup," are widely available by diving into an ocean of world music. Our pool is no longer limited to the music of our own nation or religious tradition.

At one time, such an approach would have been branded heretical. The westernized concept of the sacred was once restricted to formal religious traditions, orchestrated by clergy. In the modern age, Western theology gradually supplemented religious beliefs with the lessons of science and psychology. This resulted in the rise of liberal theology, which questioned the idea of ultimate truth in religion but still remained focused on Judeo-Christian beliefs, excluding most other religious tenets.

In the latter part of the twentieth century, the postmodern era introduced the notion that all ideas must be interpreted or evaluated in light of the surrounding culture. Belief in the ultimacy of our experiences and conclusions has been replaced with an awareness that everything is relative, even the truth. In his book *Faith Without Certainty*, Paul Rasor writes, "What we used to think of as truth is now seen as interpretation."

Postmodern thought continues to blur our cultural boundaries in food, dress, music, and even religion. It has resulted in syncretism—the reconciliation or fusion of differing systems of belief. In *Postmodernity*, David Lyon describes the results of syncretism: "New possibilities emerge, creating liturgical smorgasbords, doctrinal potlucks. As the sacred canopy recedes and the floating signs multiply, the problem becomes less 'how do I conform?' and more 'how do I choose?'" Singing meditation invites singers to feast at this liturgical smorgasbord.

Syncretism and the move away from traditional mainstream religions have broadened our definition of sacred music. Archeology, anthropology, and the ease of audio recording combine with the power of the Internet to put a vast array of music—from Sumerian hymns etched into clay tablets to present day Wiccan rituals—literally at our fingertips. The availability of this diverse music has made it possible for spiritual practices to become more inclusive.

Respecting Other Cultures

As we embrace and explore the sacred music associated with other beliefs, the religious landscape begins to soften and run together like the edges of a watercolor. We begin to lose the solid lines that once divided us. Speaking at a forum on world culture, ethnomusicologist Bruno Nettl has observed that people of all religions create music as a means of communicating with God. He sees music as a gateway to better understanding other religions and cultures. It can be the unifying factor in creating and coloring the landscape of our spiritual lives.

The term *appropriation* can mean borrowing or using practices from other cultures or traditions. This is not necessarily improper. If done respectfully, the practice can enhance the spiritual nature of worship and programs. However, appropriation's evil twin, *misappropriation*, results when the practices of a particular culture are misused or misinterpreted. Even when done inadvertently, it can evoke pain or discomfort in others.

When we experience something new and memorable, whether visiting an exotic location or attending a theatrical performance, we often want some souvenir or keepsake to validate the experience. A CD of an original cast recording or a tee shirt from the Grand Canyon not only revives a pleasant memory for us, but also allows us to share that experience with others. It may also increase our esteem among others, serving as a measure of our "coolness." Promotional tee shirts and CDs are designed for this purpose.

This concept can also apply to experiences that represent a particular heritage or culture. It's natural to be drawn to experiences that are distinctive, such as dance or music from another culture. We may enjoy or be moved by a ceremony or performance, even if we don't completely understand the tradition or culture that created the event. But our involvement with the event becomes misappropriation when we re-create the experience to exploit it for our own benefit.

When the Shades of Praise gospel choir visited St. Paul, Minnesota, we had the glorious experience of attending their performance. This interracial choir, based in New Orleans, was invited to the city as part of a program to explore links between historically black and white churches. In St. Paul, as in many American cities, racial tensions hum beneath the surface but are difficult to discuss openly. While both black and white churches decry racism, they have been uncertain how to move forward to build bridges or create partnerships.

Shades of Praise was electrifying. They sang an hour of pure, joyful praise music. The audience, interracial and interfaith, rose to its feet, clapping and swaying and shouting, "Amen." Their response conformed to instructions written by Horace Clarence Boyer in his preface to *Lift Every Voice and Sing II: An African American Hymnal*. He suggested that gospel singing should be accompanied by rhythmic movements such as "hand clapping, patting the feet, swaying, nodding the head, raising the arms upward, and shouting of the body" to better align the singer with worshiping.

No one present at that worship service could have remained unmoved. The music insinuated itself into us in a wonderful way, seeming to transcend race and religion. It proclaimed universal truths: *I have a soul, you have a soul, God is the light, let him flip your switch!* The worship service was an experience of pure, absolute love and joy.

Yet we found ourselves wondering: Do the choir members assume that the audience's enthusiastic response implies not "soul meeting soul" but "Christian meeting Christian"? There were many Unitarian Universalists in the crowd that night—some of them humanists and atheists—and at least one Buddhist monk wearing a burgundy and saffron robe. Most of the audience, including the monk, raised their hands in joy to acknowledge the singers. Yet we know that in some fundamentalist groups, raising your hand when someone sings "Jesus healed my wounds" means you accept and embrace that statement, that it's true for you too. It's doubtful that many of the "unsaved" in the crowd realized this. Does that mean they were wrong to raise their hands in joy? Does it mean they were not entitled to share in the powerful message of this music?

If we had polled each choir member that night, we might have heard a dozen different responses to these questions. It is difficult to say who owns a musical heritage, or who has the right to share it with others. Looked at in a cynical way, the choir's visit to St. Paul might be considered as bait that lured two disparate communities into coming together. Enjoying a community dinner after the performance, watching people from many churches and backgrounds get acquainted, we concluded that the end justified the means.

Singing as a Universal Impulse

When we borrow songs from other traditions in singing meditation sessions, we treat them as invited guests. We extend to them our full attention and hospitality. We understand that we are tapping into the universal use of music as spiritual expression, a tradition found on every continent and in every heritage.

Although singing meditation as a spiritual practice is quite young and still evolving, its genesis lies in this universal impulse to sing in community. Song as celebration is emblematic of the human condition. Song as leitmotif to the sacred is as old as the caves that once sheltered our ancestors. Since the dawn of civilization, humans have used sound and music to celebrate life, explain its mysteries, and transcend the human experience.

In a conversation with Keith Arnold, minister of music at Jefferson Unitarian Church in Colorado, we attempted to define *sacred music*. We quickly agreed on a traditional definition—that sacred music addresses or talks about God—but this definition seemed incomplete. Keith, a music scholar, began to elaborate about several sacred musical forms but soon broke off, realizing that they didn't quite answer the question either.

"Sacred music," he finally said, "is any music that reminds us we are alive. Regardless of its subject matter, any music can lift us. At its best, music enriches, inspires, and entreats us to change our lives."

This definition is a good starting point. However, when music is used as part of a worship service, its spiritual message generally connects with and reinforces a theological one. Church musicians and clergy rely on theological bedrock to inform their final choice of music for a service. In a 2007 sermon, Christopher Edmonston, a Presbyterian minister, reflects on the role of song this way: "Is there anything more indicative of the human life, more unique to the human experience, more necessary to the Christian faith and to the expression of our joy before God than the singing of song, the praise we offer through hymn, carol, or anthem?"

Early Christian music involved chanting the Psalms and gradually expanded to more elaborate melodies and other Bible verses. It eventually became so complex that the Council of Trent, convened in the sixteenth century to address issues facing the Roman Catholic Church, created new rules for sacred music. They decreed that sacred music must be dignified and serious and, above all, understandable so that members of the congregation could participate fully in singing praise to God.

This distinction between participating in chant or sung prayer and passive listening is important. The tone and vibration of the music itself activate something physiological that brings inner harmony and quiets the mind. In Hindu spiritual practice, for example, the act of chanting is considered as important as the meaning of the chant itself. Sanskrit Hindu chants are directed to the specific *deva*, or aspect of God, that will be most helpful in a given situation. A chant to Ganesha, considered the remover of obstacles, may be offered to ensure success in a new project. The goddess Durga (or Kali), considered the protector of our moral order, is invoked as protection from suffering and evil. Practitioners believe that both the words chanted and the vibrations of the chant induce a positive effect on the chanter.

Rabbi Michael Lerner, founder and chair of the Network of Spiritual Progressives, believes in the transformative power of joyful music in the religious life. Song and dance in the synagogue help worshipers celebrate the universe and the potential to be God's partner in healing and transforming the world. Lerner says, "For us, singing and dancing are not ways to achieve something else—they are a central part of expressing who we are in the moment of our transcendence of the demands of 'the real world' as we reconnect to the God who is the Possibility of Possibility, the 'I Shall Be Who I Shall Be,' the Force that breaks the repetition compulsion and allows us to move toward our fullest being."

When music becomes an active agent in a spiritual practice, becoming a manifestation of the divine rather than simply a carrier of praise or supplication, the experience is often called "ecstatic." In his encyclopedic study, *Sacred Song in America: Religion, Music, and Public Culture*, Stephen Marini explains how the call-and-response songs of African-American churches act as a manifestation of the divine. Specifically, they reflect the capricious nature of the sacred in African-American traditions, what Marini calls the "free play and vitality inherent in the sacred itself." The musical form of call and response employs two elements: one that is fixed (the chorus) and one that is improvised (the soloist). The juxtaposition of fixed and free, text and music, manifests the sacred. Marini notes, "Both call and response are necessary to articulate this spiritual reality because the sacred can neither be captured by form nor be experienced without form."

Even if the music or chant itself is not transcendent, bringing us to an ecstatic place, it can still serve as a pointer, leading us toward that possibility. The music is a vehicle to change our mood. It can awaken us from boredom or weariness, or it can calm our anxieties and bring inner peace.

Monsignor George Ratzinger, conductor of the Cathedral Choir of Regensburg, Germany, writes in *Frequently Asked Questions on Sacred Music*, "Liturgical music must lead towards prayer and meditation. It has to calm one, to enable one to concentrate on God, on the essential." Ratzinger's older brother, Joseph Cardinal Ratzinger (now Pope Bendedict XVI) in the same publication reflects on the use of music in the Catholic Mass: "Does it not do us good, before we set off into the center of the mystery, to encounter a short time... in which the choir calms us... leading each one of us into silent prayer?" The choir's song eases us into a place of contemplation and allows us to listen deeply for the sound of God's voice.

In his article, "On Appreciation of Indian Classical Music," Indian musician Ravi Shankar writes that music itself is a "spiritual discipline on the path to self-realization. By this process individual consciousness can be elevated to a realm of awareness where the revelation of the true meaning of the universe—its eternal and unchanging essence—can be joyfully experienced." Zacciah Blackburn, co-founder of the World Sound Healing Organization, says in "The Power of Chant" that chants are "doorways or portals to unlimited resources.... Through our desire to purify our own thought and action, we couple with the purified (rarified) essence of the Divine, opening ourselves to its unlimited bounty."

Sacred music may lead to a direct experience of the divine or at least point in the right direction. It may transmit a message or provide an opportunity to form an ephemeral community with others that is sacred within itself. On any given day, the same song may provide one or more of these experiences—or none. No music can guarantee that the singer or chanter will achieve ecstasy or mystical union with the divine. But song's universal ability to calm, open, and elevate our minds and spirits happens often enough to be celebrated by nearly every spiritual tradition.

According to the Upanishads, Brahma created the world by chanting the syllable *om*, a sound formed by merging the three letters A, U, and M. Many meanings are applied to this word, including "all the names of God," "all aspects of God," and "the everlasting and unceasing tone." To this day, devotees of some of India's religions chant *om* to create a vibration in sympathy with the cosmic vibration, and believe the sound represents all possible sounds—and therefore, all possible prayers—that can be enunciated by humans.

Ancient Greeks considered the god Hermes to be the founder of music. As early as the sixth century BCE, he was named as the creator of the first lyre and shepherd's flute. The ancient Greeks also believed music had power over the human soul and human behavior. Plato thought that nothing influenced human feelings more strongly than melody and rhythm, and that only gods or godlike humans could compose inspirational music. Pythagoras claimed the soul could be purified by music sung to the accompaniment of the lyre.

Buddhist sacred chant goes back to the time of the Buddha himself. Tibetan Buddhist chant is so integral to religious life that the lamas say simply, "Religion is sound." Chinese Buddhists brought chant to Japan around 719 CE. Chanting dominated the life of Buddhist monks during this time; scripture lecturing was performed in chants, and all official functions involved long, complicated chants. Chant, recitation of mantras, and instrumental music remain important aspects of Buddhist practice.

Some Native American cultures believe that music originated from deities. The Pima people, for example, believe many of their ritual songs were originally sung by their creator. Hopi legends say Spider Woman brought life to inanimate forms by singing songs over them.

Australian aboriginals sing an intricate series of songs called songlines to relate creation stories and pass down navigational landmarks from one generation to the next. Death, often viewed as the result of sorcery, necessitates the singing of songs during funerals or immediately after death to help the deceased find their place in the afterlife.

Music is mentioned in Genesis, the first book of the Bible, citing Jubal, as the father of all who play the harp and flute. Spontaneous music was common among ancient Jews. Religious music at first consisted of chanting Bible verses; later, prayers and poetry were also chanted.

Early Christian music, based on the Psalms, sought to calm and soothe human passions. Christians have used the Psalms for worship dating from at least as far back as the third century CE.

Sound versus Text

The sacred music we experience today generally has two components: music and lyrics. Sometimes these two will complement each other so well that they seem inseparable. Increasingly, however, there have been disagreements about whether a song can—or should—be enjoyed without a heartfelt endorsement of its lyrics.

Hearing the beautiful sound of the *Agnus Dei* in Latin at a Catholic Mass might move someone to tears, even if the words are not understood. Another person in the same pew may all but ignore the music and become completely absorbed in contemplation of Jesus as the Lamb of God. All is well, as long as these two don't compare notes on their spiritual approaches and are tolerant of each other's internal spiritual process. But conflict can arise when one person discovers that the message of the music that he or she considers sacred is apparently irrelevant to someone else's spiritual experience of the music.

The history of Sacred Harp singing illustrates the controversy that can erupt over the roles of the text and theology in sacred music. Church music in colonial New England consisted of singing the psalms in unison. To expand the role of sacred singing, Thomas Walter published a singing manual in 1721, and opened a school in Boston to train people in musical notation and harmony. Singing in harmony proved popular, and the practice spread throughout the United States. In the mid-1800s, several hymnbooks were published to support the newly organized evangelical camp meetings. *The Sacred Harp* hymnbook, published in 1844, used simple geometric shapes, called "shape notes," in place of standard musical notes. Although more than one hymnal using shape notes was published during this era, the terms *Sacred Harp singing* and *shape-note singing* have been nearly synonymous ever since.

After the Civil War, interest in shape-note singing waned, although it remained popular in the rural South. In the mid-1970s, Sacred Harp groups began to spring up in northern states such as New York, Wisconsin, Illinois, Oregon, Ohio, New Jersey, and Colorado. By 1999, about 40 percent of Sacred Harp groups met in locations outside the South.

Traditional Sacred Harp singing had no audience, because everyone present sang. Unaccompanied by musical instruments, it often lasted for hours. Strict born-again Christian Southerners considered the experience a form of worship. For them, the primary purpose of the singing was to convey biblical and moral teaching; fellowship was a secondary consideration. All singers were expected to believe in the same Christian doctrine.

For the new Northern singers, the songs represented communication with God, but the content of the words was less important than the feeling of fellowship, community, and extended family among the singers. The music provided a feeling of unity and ritual but did not require singers to accept a particular dogma. Some Northerners even offered public performances.

The tension between Northern and Southern singers was pronounced by the late 1980s. Southerners thought the Northerners had subtracted the fundamental religious teachings from the songs and, therefore, were not singing for the right reasons. They felt the new singers had objectified the music and made it a commodity by performing it for audiences; they had trivialized the spiritual underpinnings of the music by turning it into entertainment.

Today, the two groups are amicable, but they are aware of their differences. Both sides agree that Sacred Harp singing is a powerful agent for creating fellowship among singers. Southern singers object, however, when fellowship and singing occur without embracing the fundamentalist Christian doctrine in the lyrics.

Concern about whether text or sound should be most important did not originate with the singers of Sacred Harp music. It goes back at least to the fourth century. St. Augustine, a stickler for the supremacy of text over sound, observed that melody had the potential to overpower the message it was meant to deliver. In his *Confessions*, he wrote, "I am inclined to approve of the custom of singing in church, in order that by indulging the ears weaker spirits may be inspired with feeling of devotion. Yet when I find the singing itself more moving than the truth which it conveys, I confess that this is a grievous sin, and at those times I would prefer not to hear the singer."

When the role of a sacred song is to educate, the text naturally takes priority over the melody. Gregorian chant, known today for its beauty and complexity, began in the sixth or seventh century as a monastic practice of chanting liturgical texts. Its main purpose is to faithfully convey the words and meaning of sacred text. Singers clearly enunciate the Latin words and are urged to understand and contemplate their meaning before attempting to chant.

Some Buddhist chants relate the stories and teachings of the Buddha. These chants instruct as well as prepare the mind for meditation. Buddhist chant originated in India, adapting to local custom and need as it spread throughout the East. Many of these adaptations made reciting and understanding the meaning and lesson of the chants easier for ordinary people.

At the opposite end of the spectrum from the "text is supreme" viewpoint are the Hasidic Jews. The founder of the Hasidic movement in the eighteenth century, Rabbi Israel Baal Shem Tov, taught that joy should permeate one's relationship with God. Singing creates a connection between God and humanity, and words are

viewed as obstacles to this connection. People can attain the ultimate union with God by singing wordless melodies.

Inspired by their desire to connect with God, the Hasidim
composed a body of music referred to collectively as *nigunim* (sin-
gular *nigun*). Almost all nigunim are wordless and typically are sung
a cappella. They are organized into three main categories: *dveykes*,
to promote communion with God; *tish*, sung after holiday or Sabbath meals; and dance tunes sung in unison. Instead of using text,
the Hasidim invented a group of vocalized syllables that could be
sung with great emotion and energy. Syllables such as *bim bam*, *ay
ay ay*, or *oy vey* are sung in no specific order or pattern, leaving the
singer free to vocalize as he or she feels moved.

In his article "Nigun," Rabbi Tzvi Freeman describes the practice this way: "With a nigun, what is held imprisoned deep in the
soul pours down into the mind and from the mind to the heart…
a nigun can uplift and transform all of your being… song carries
the soul upwards to be absorbed within the Infinite Light." Nigun
singers, in contrast to the Sacred Harp singers of the southern
United States, are perfectly willing to dispense with words altogether and let the spirit manifest itself as it will.

Singing meditation groups are created without a bedrock theology so they can more easily be embraced by people of many
spiritual beliefs. Therefore sound, not text, is the most important
aspect of the songs that work best. Freeman's article notes that this
perspective aligns with the belief of Rabbi Menachem Mendal,
who taught, "When words are spoken we each hear the words according to our understanding. But in song, we are all united in a
single pulse and a single melody."

Sometimes, the right words augment the spiritual effect of the
music both by their actual meaning and the additional qualities of
the sound induced by singing those particular words. For example,
if a singer believes deeply that the earth is our mother and that
we have a duty to protect her, the singer's resonance while singing these words—"The Earth is our mother, we must take care of
her"—will add a richer dimension to the song.

Our personal understanding of what is sacred naturally colors our view of how it relates to singing. Spirituality is a universal impulse toward phenomena that are difficult to define or discuss. Singing, wordlessly or with text, offers a unique way to plumb the depths of our spirituality. It may represent the communion between man and the Supreme Being, as composer Igor Stravinsky discovered. Or as cellist Pablo Casals suggested, singing is a private way to "tell beautiful, poetic things to the heart." The metaphors we create to describe our own experiences will be as unique as our thumbprints.

At a typical singing meditation session, we may sing a Jewish round followed by a Christian song in four-part harmony, and then move on to a Sufi song or a Buddhist chant. Each expresses a universal longing for the divine, a desire to reach beyond our individual egos into something infinite.

While it is beyond the scope of this book to include background on each and every song that has been or will ever be sung in singing meditation, we will discuss three vibrant contemporary spiritual practices whose songs are used often in sessions—Taizé prayer, kirtan call-and-repeat chants, and Dances of Universal Peace.

Taizé

Taizé is a contemplative worship service based on short chants and songs, interspersed with Christian scripture, prayer, and silence. The Taizé community originated in southern France in 1940, when Roger Louis Schutz-Marsauche, a Swiss Protestant minister, came to the hamlet of Taizé seeking solitude and prayer. Brother Roger's home soon became a refuge for Jews fleeing the Nazis. After the war, others who shared his vision of a simple, prayerful life in an ecumenical setting joined him. The community now includes more than a hundred Protestant and Catholic brothers from twenty-five nations.

The ministry of Taizé has focused on young adults aged eighteen to thirty. Today the retreat center attracts thousands of young people annually from around the world. These pilgrims seek the opportunity to share community and spiritual connection with others. Participants arrive on Sunday for a week-long retreat. They live simply, sitting on wooden benches and taking light meals together outdoors. They participate in daily prayer services and scripture-focused workshops intended to deepen the relationship between faith and life in the areas of work, social questions, art and culture, and the search for world peace. On Friday, the evening service includes veneration of the cross, a ceremony during which participants pay respect to the crucifix by kneeling and praying, or kissing the foot of the cross. This ritual originated in Jerusalem in the fourth century with the adoration of a wood fragment believed to be from the original cross. At Taizé, the ritual becomes a vigil that caps the retreat.

Since the 1980s, the brothers have been engaged in a worldwide pilgrimage of reconciliation to bring together Christians throughout the world. The community's work with the poor in Asia, South America, and Africa aligns with their purpose of encouraging followers to put the Taizé spirit into practice in their local communities.

Chris Walton, editor of the Unitarian Universalist magazine *UU World*, traveled to Taizé in 2005. He describes his visit as an extraordinary experience, a pleasant surprise to him as an American religious liberal. He found a true community that welcomed everyone. In an interview, he said, "Their extraordinary commitment to hospitality is embodied in the way they run the monastery and their charitable work." The Taizé brothers welcome spiritual seekers. "We met several who came simply because Taizé is the one place they knew in Europe where their spiritual quest would be taken seriously, generously, and without judgment," Walton continued. "The Brothers have a way of teaching that is incredibly leveling."

Music is an integral part of the daily prayer services at Taizé. The songs usually consist of a short, simple phrase repeated several times. Unlike Gregorian chant, which is sung without accompaniment, Taizé compositions include instrumentation. During services, songs may be sung in several languages, sometimes simultaneously, to honor and reflect the diversity of participants, and Taizé songbooks include multiple translations for each song. The songs are repeated several times, creating a prayerful, contemplative atmosphere that allows the meaning of the text to be fully absorbed without conscious effort.

Prayer services are held three times daily. A typical service includes:

- One or two songs sung in a slow, meditative style.
- A short scripture, often a psalm. The text can be either spoken or sung.
- A single long period of silence, from five to ten minutes, in which to contemplate the scripture or other spiritual questions.
- Prayer of intercession or thanksgiving.
- Additional meditative songs.

During evening services, flickering candles provide dim light. The focus is on the individual's connection with God rather than with others. The brothers lead the service from the center of the sanctuary. "This orientation opens a kind of vulnerability that helps the worshipers center in a deep place," Walton explains. He notes that this individual approach is always practiced during prayer service. At other times, however, community sharing is very much encouraged, especially discussion about becoming agents of change in the world. "The monks of Taizé use their music as an initial spark to get people more interested in their mission and service work. The monks realize that the primary appeal is aesthetic—the music is beautiful and moving, and though its liturgical intention is not obvious to most people at first, the music is always relevant to the liturgy. It amplifies the liturgical moment."

In *Reinventing Sunday*, Brad Berglund, a pastor and musician who teaches workshops on Taizé-style worship, describes his first experience with Taizé singing: "Singers began adding choral parts until all four parts wrapped around my soul as a cloak. As I sang in that community of musicians, I prayed in a way I'd never prayed before."

Taizé music has now become a focal point of popular Taizé-style services held regularly in many denominations, including Roman Catholic, Methodist, Episcopal, Presbyterian, and Lutheran. When the Taizé brothers visited Montreal in 2006 for a youth event, they discovered that the Chinese Catholic community there had been praying Taizé songs in Mandarin for several years. Taizé makes its music available on CDs, MP3s, and in songbooks, so it can be used in services anywhere in the world. They have published guidelines for holding local services that honor the basic format of those at the Taizé community. The guidelines contain practical recommendations for leading the group, such as holding practice sessions separately from worship service to allow everyone to become comfortable with songs ahead of time.

Taizé prayers are well suited for the practice described in this book—they are contemplative, short, and easy to learn. Some are written as rounds and others as chants; many are arranged in four-part harmony. Singing these beautiful prayers repetitively in a group is deeply satisfying.

Singing meditation sessions are different from Taizé prayer services in several ways. The Taizé community does not hold silence between each song. Their services are more likely to hold only one long interval of silent prayer. Taizé includes spoken prayer, while prayer in our practice is silent. Both types of gatherings include readings, but the Bible is the only source in Taizé practice. Inspirational readings can be drawn from several sources during singing meditation.

Kirtan

Kirtan is the communal singing and chanting of devotional songs and sacred hymns. Kirtan is Sanskrit for "repeat," and today the term is used to refer both to individual chants and songs as well as to the act of gathering to share the practice or listen to the sacred music. Although its roots lie in India, kirtan carries no link to a specific religion. For clearer identification, groups gathering today to sing Hindu-based songs may call themselves "Hindu Kirtan," while those gathering to sing Hebrew words are called "Hebrew Kirtan."

Although they represent only a fraction of the types of music used in singing meditation, call-and-repeat songs are the type of kirtan music most often included in the practice. During call-and-repeat kirtan sessions, a leader calls a portion of the chant, and participants respond by repeating it. The intention is to transport participants to the spiritual realm through the vibrations and sounds of the chant, and in the process to quiet the mind and open the heart. Dave Stringer has developed a kirtan style that blends Eastern and Western music. In his article "Kirtan," he writes, "The intention of kirtan is consciousness-transformative, directing the singers to vanish into the song as drops merge into the ocean. The musicians and the crowd coalesce in a cloud of intelligence, turning together like a flock of birds, until the song itself vanishes into the blue skies of silence."

Kirtan was first introduced to mainstream American culture through the Hare Krishna chants popularized in the 1970s. Kirtan is practiced in the Sikh, Hindu, and Sufi traditions. In the West, kirtans are often held in conjunction with yoga practice. The call-and-repeat format is easy for participants to learn and so it is a good choice for singing meditation practice.

Andrew Wilke, who has led and practiced kirtan in Wisconsin since 2000, believes that kirtan makes the divine more accessible by "collecting and synchronizing individual experience. In much the same way that there is awe engendered by a school of fish all collectively snapping to a new direction, there is something equally profound in experiencing the 'tightness' in intonation, breath, and rhythm of kirtan."

The roots of kirtan reach back more than five hundred years to India. During that period, Brahmin priests carefully guarded Sanskrit mantras as a commodity bought and sold by warlords seeking military or commercial success. Kirtan allowed ordinary people to participate in music and worship, removing the need for a priest to serve as an intermediary to or interpreter of God. As Wilke explains, "Fundamentally, [Kirtan] was a rebellion against the pathological usurping of exclusive access to God by the Brahmin priests. We in the West are only now beginning to experience this very healthy reclamation of direct access to God."

In Sikh kirtan, singing is accompanied by the *tala*, a very specific rhythmic pattern repeated over and over. The model is based on ancient *ragas*. A raga is a set of rules used to build a melody so that the pattern of the notes is recognizable yet variable. There is a raga for each time of day, and every raga connects to a specific mood or feeling—for instance, joy, happiness, satisfaction, or grief.

Kirtan chants often express love for the divine. In the Sikh tradition, the source of the hymns is the *Guru Granth Sahib*, the holy book that contains the words spoken by the Sikh gurus. Sikh kirtan practice follows very specific rules. Each hymn must be sung to the correct raga and tala. Certain songs may not be interrupted; others are required or disallowed at particular times of day. Correct pronunciation and intonation of the words is important so the audience can understand the meaning of the hymn. No lectures on the text are permitted. Flashy displays of musical skills are discouraged, because they tend to distract the minds of the singers. Once begun, a hymn must be completed, which may take twenty to thirty minutes. For those accustomed to our fast-paced sound-byte mentality, kirtan is a new concept.

Sufi kirtan, known as *qawwali*, has similarly strict rules for listening and performing, designed to ensure that music leads to spiritual growth rather than indulging the desire for pleasure and enjoyment. The qawwali ritual is more performance than participation, gathering listeners to inspire them with the words of Islamic mystics.

In American culture, kirtan practice generally follows more relaxed rules. Jai Uttal, a performer and recording artist who has gained notoriety as a kirtan singer, said in a radio interview about his practice, "It doesn't have to be fancy, it doesn't have to be super musical, it just has to be truthful."

Leaders often find that the group's response helps shape the arc of the kirtan. It may begin slowly, but the group's energy causes it to gradually increase in tempo before slowing again. Besides reflecting the group's physical energy, the tempo metaphorically represents the rise and fall of the spiritual experience.

As in singing meditation, a kirtan leader must be confident enough in the musical presentation to help participants learn unfamiliar music. Wilke, who has experienced both practices, explains: "One needs to know when to steer and when to allow the autopilot feature to take over. If this happens, a momentum gathers that quickly relegates musical prowess to a secondary position below the outstretched hands of joy." For him, the most enjoyable kirtan combines "musical skill with humble, yet intense, meditative awareness and listening on the part of the leader."

Whether or not the chant leads to blissful spiritual heights, the act of committing to sing and chant together has value. Although each person strives for an individual level of spiritual connection and mindfulness, sharing the experience deepens and enhances the sense of connection to each other and to the divine.

Dances of Universal Peace

Dances of Universal Peace are a spiritual practice that unites sacred movement, song, and story from many world traditions. The dances, performed in a sacred setting, evoke deep feelings and promote a sense of connection among participants. They focus on peace and harmony, and celebrate the underlying unity of all spiritual traditions to increase our appreciation and understanding of our own and other cultures.

The practice is not a performance but a participatory experience. The songs are short and the dance steps simple. Changing partners during a dance is often choreographed into the steps. Participants need no prior experience in dance or music and may attend without a partner.

The first Peace Dances were created in the 1960s by Samuel L. Lewis, a Sufi teacher and Rinzai Zen master who had studied a number of world religions. Lewis's vision was to promote peace through the arts. He was influenced by his studies with both Hazrat Inayat Khan, the teacher who first brought Sufism to the West, and Ruth St. Denis, an American dancer who was one of the first to incorporate Eastern spiritual elements into Western dance.

Initially, the dances were part of the Sufi Islamia Ruhaniat Society, whose authorization and training were required before the dances could be publicly shared. In 1982, the International Network for the Dances of Universal Peace was formed, deliberately separating the practice from this Sufi order to allow the dances to be more widely shared. The Network is the communication hub for the dances. It maintains a registry of certified dance leaders, archives recognized songs and dances, and sponsors workshops and events. Because the original dances came from the Sufi tradition, you may occasionally hear these dances referred to as "Sufi dancing."

The original body of about fifty dances has now grown to more than five hundred, taught in many countries worldwide. The dances are drawn from Hinduism, Buddhism, Zoroastrianism, Sikhism, Judaism, Christianity, and Islam, as well as the Aramaic, Native American, Native Middle Eastern, Hawaiian, Celtic, Native African, and Goddess traditions. They celebrate the mystery of life and themes of peace and healing.

John Hakim Bushnell, who has led the practice in Minnesota since 1990, explained that new dances develop when their creator begins to have a meditative relationship with the name of God or a spiritual phrase that speaks to him or her. He said, "Then you tone on one note until you let the name have control—until it is doing you, not you doing it." Only in this expansive mode can the creator approach the melody. After becoming familiar with the melody through practice, the creator can begin to consider the dance.

To become a certified leader, one must work with a mentor who is already certified. Certification requires at least three years of study and a relationship with one sacred or spiritual path or tradition, although no particular tradition is required. Leaders demonstrate the ability to convey an appropriate sacred atmosphere as well as "attunement," described by the Network for the Dances of Universal Peace as "the willingness and ability, while leading, to attune and surrender to the blessing transmitted through the Dances." Leaders and mentors agree to respect the integrity of the original dances, although innovation is expected in order to accommodate specific groups of dancers.

Live music, including percussion, stringed instruments, and flutes, often accompanies the dances. In a typical session, dancers form a circle around the leader and musicians. Choreography calls for frequent changes of partner to encourage contact with several people in the course of a session. The leader teaches the lyrics, music, and movements for each dance, usually including some background about the dance or the tradition from which it is drawn. Because many of the songs include non-English lyrics, leaders repeat the words until people are comfortable with pronunciation. After each dance, the leader may have the group hold the circle formation and honor a brief period of silence.

According to Hakim, the vibration of the song is central to the dance; the vibration is "right" when the prayer or song is in its original language. He notes, "The sacred phrase or name of God is the center of the Dance. If you got rid of everything else, that would still have a mystical effect." Hakim began his experience with the dances as a guitarist, so he was especially attuned to its music. He believes the "sound" of the dance is critical to its success. As a leader, he tries for "the Dionysian experience with an

Apollonian foundation. When participants focus attention, there is an unspoken, expansive effect that intensifies the experience." He adds, however, that it is perfectly acceptable to just soak or bask in the music or movement.

Stephen Brown, who has practiced the Dances since 1981, found them to be an "awakening experience." He enjoys the combination of movement and music as a fluid spiritual practice, as well as the interaction with other dancers. "This interaction supports the Sufi concept of fully living in the world, rather than being a hermit or meditating in a cave." Hakim agrees that this "group consciousness" is an important part of the practice, because when people really hear each other, they can move toward transcendence. He facilitates this process by instructing the group to sing more loudly or softly, or by alternating singing by men and women.

The flow of the session and choice of songs is flexible, changing in response to the group energy. A leader may prepare a dance set but almost always modifies it, depending on the experience level of the participating dancers. Leaders need a repertoire of at least thirty dances to mix and match, according to the needs of a particular group.

Perry Pike, who has led the practice since 1996, refers to the energy of the dance space as organic. "People dance their joy, their grief, their pain. I do this not to dance a 'pretty' dance but a dance that says I am alive." The practice promotes an atmosphere of intercultural connection and peace. Joining hands, singing together, and dancing in a circle creates a sense of real connection and community.

The repertoires of Dances of Universal Peace and singing meditation are more similar to each other than they are to the other practices discussed in this chapter. Like that of singing meditation, the dance repertoire is eclectic and inclusive of many spiritual paths. The main differences between the two practices are that the dance practice only rarely includes silence for meditation between songs and, while singing meditation may include sacred dancing, it is usually not the focus of a session.

Singing meditation is based on the belief that many paths can lead to spiritual growth, renewal, and understanding. The songs we use represent vastly different religious traditions, but they share one important characteristic: Each provides a prism through which we can examine our understanding of self and its relationship to others. The more we understand the cultural contexts and religious impulses inherent in a song, the more facets the prism contains to catch and reflect the light of collective experience.

Silence and Spirituality

Many people who find joy in singing prefer to postpone or avoid the silent periods of singing meditation, at least at first. Music, not silence, attracts them. Those who can burst into song at the drop of a hat often wait impatiently through the silence for the next song to begin. Their love of singing keeps them involved, despite the enforced silences. Yet among this group, many eventually come to cherish the silence between the songs as well.

Others discover immediately that the shared periods of silence enhance the experience. After attending just two sessions, Margee reflected, "For me, the silence after each song heightens the experience, makes the singing meditation special in a way that would not be true if we only sang the songs together. In terms of it being a spiritual experience, the silence is key. It allows the song to linger and lets me experience whatever arises from the singing—prayerful visualizations, gratefulness, or simply being at peace in the moment."

There is a qualitative difference between silence that happens merely because sound is absent and silence cultivated by "presence." The juxtaposition of song and silence creates a space for contemplation. The silence is enhanced by the vibrations of the song that precedes it. Patty, a singing meditation practitioner, says the silence lets her "absorb and appreciate the subtle reverberations of the act of singing together. One image I have is that of a big bell or cymbal being struck. It's easy to notice that initial loud gong and go right on to the next thing. But if you stay quiet and really follow the sound, it actually goes on and on and on, changing nature until its reverberations finally diminish into a wonderful stillness. I appreciate the stillness all the more because it is shared. We've started from a common source (the words and tones of a song), followed the reverberations, and found quietness together. There's a completeness about it that can be missed if you just jump from song to song."

Personal choice dictates how participants use the intervals of silence. Singing meditation operates on the premise that there are many paths to God, both with its repertoire of songs and its use of the silence that frames them. The teachings and examples of spiritual silence fall into three broad categories: meditation, prayer, and contemplation.

Meditation

With the introduction of Eastern religions into Western culture, the practice of meditation has grown popular. Meditation relaxes the body and focuses the mind until it becomes empty of thought, allowing us to become fully present. With practice, meditation trains the mind to stay focused on truth in any situation, no matter what emotions we feel or what events may occur. It involves anchoring our thoughts to something, such as the breath itself, prayers, a repeated word or mantra, or a poem or spiritual text. This practice helps us tame the "wild creature" of our mind.

People new to meditation may fret or give up completely because their thoughts run rampant, and they fail to achieve the goal of emptying their minds. We need to remember that thoughts and outside distractions naturally occur whenever we try to still our minds. It is not realistic to expect that sitting in silence will result in a blissful, empty mind on the first—or the hundredth—attempt. In meditation, the goal is to simply notice these distractions and release them without getting attached to them. Then we can return to the focus of attention.

Meditation practice can take many forms. Some repeat a mantra or sacred word as a signal or symbol to connect the person with God or Spirit. The mantras in some practices are lengthy and complex, causing some people concern about proper pronunciation. Spiritual teacher Swami Sivananda Radha, founder of the Association for the Development of Human Potential, addresses this concern in *Mantras: Words of Power*: "Your sincerity and what is in your heart and mind are more important than the pronunciation. There are thousands of people who pronounce words correctly but they have not yet become saints."

People who regularly meditate report many benefits: a feeling of peace, increased ability to focus, and a host of other results. Although these outcomes might not be directly measurable, they certainly contribute to overall health and well-being.

A friend who practices meditation credits it with helping him to quickly re-center himself after learning of the events of September 11, 2001. He was shocked and horrified, as we all were, but was able to focus his mind on loving thoughts to quell his fears. He was able to connect with others and spread a feeling of calm and peace rather than panic.

Hallie Moore is a poet and teacher who practices passage meditation as part of the Eight Point Program, a spiritual practice developed by Eknath Easwaran. Passage meditation is silent, focused repetition of memorized selections from the scriptures of world religions and the writings of mystics. As she works one-on-one with students, Moore finds that her meditation practice deepens her understanding and helps her to be more sensitive and flexible in her approach. Because meditation has improved her self-discipline, she is better able to empathize with the challenges her students face and to hold her own when she needs to be firm. "I'm always struck by the mystery of meditation," she told the newsletter of the Blue Mountain Center of Meditation. "I don't know exactly how it works. I just know that if I keep at it, my life stays pretty stable, without the drama, but with all the bright colors."

Prayer

Christian theologians have described two approaches to prayer: cataphatic and apophatic. *Cataphatic* prayer uses words, images, nature, and the senses to bring one to a closer experience with God. In *apophatic* prayer, which includes centering and contemplation, one empties oneself of words and images, which are considered inadequate to connect with or describe the divine. Neither form is considered superior. At different times in our spiritual lives, we may find comfort with one or the other approach. Apophatic prayer perhaps requires us to "go deeper" in an esoteric way, while in cataphatic prayer, we use sensory input to turn our attention to the divine.

Singing sacred songs can be a cataphatic form of prayer, the beauty of the music and language pointing the way to communion with God. The silent periods between songs can be used for apophatic prayer or, if preferred, for additional cataphatic prayer in the form of unspoken words.

Parallels between singing meditation and the flow of monastic life include the rhythm of work and prayer. Both include a balance between activity and reflection. The activity of learning the songs in singing meditation takes concentration and focus. By repeating the songs and learning them well enough to relax, we can move into a holy place of reflection and transformation.

When invited to use a time of silence for prayer, many of us have no idea where to begin. We sometimes forget how simple a prayer can be. Theologian Meister Eckhart wrote, "If the only prayer you say in your whole life is 'thank you,' that would suffice." In her book *Traveling Mercies,* writer Anne Lamott expands on this concept; the two best prayers she knows are "Help me, help me, help me," and "Thank you, thank you, thank you." These words remind us that prayer need not be complicated. *Prayer* is a broad term for any action that seeks communication between humans and the divine. In his book *Simply Pray,* Unitarian Universalist minister Erik Walker Wikstrom describes prayer as a process and an opening that allows us to "connect and reconnect to the source of our lives."

Prayer is the act of reaching out to something greater than ourselves in order to connect deeply to the source of life, the great mystery of which we are all a part and which none of us can comprehend. Prayer may involve requests and petitions, expressions of gratitude or despair, or the act of opening a channel for guidance.

Wikstrom outlines four aspects of prayer:

- Naming—understanding and giving a name (even a metaphorical one) to the force to which we wish to connect
- Knowing—which allows us to reflect on our lives as they are now, including aspects of ourselves we want to change or improve
- Listening—holding the silence to hear what is deep within us
- Loving—directing our prayer outward into the world to effect positive change.

Prayer can be considered an opportunity to open a dialog or communication channel. "Prayer is not designed to change God, but to change us," Catholic theologian Thomas Keating writes in his book *Open Mind, Open Heart*.

Prayers recited over and over during childhood may be imprinted in our memories. Unfortunately, these prayers can be so familiar that their words no longer evoke spiritual feelings. When praying familiar prayers (or singing familiar songs) it may help to notice which words catch your attention and reflect on them.

Memorized prayers have a way of activating primal memories, an almost archetypal connection to ancient rituals. A friend raised as a Roman Catholic lovingly recalls her Irish grandmother's lilt when reciting the rosary—to this day, she feels a mysterious and sacred power just holding a string of rosary beads. Groups may recite the rosary in a call-and-response format. The rhythm of the prayers sounds musical, although they are not actually sung. This ritual has the same mesmerizing effects as a chant.

Many of us learned to practice petitionary, or intercessory, prayer as children. This kind of prayer asks God for direct intervention in our world or lives, such as, "Please God, help me pass my math test." Theologians, scholars, and scientific researchers still debate the merits of such prayer. Intercessory prayer requires a faith that many people find hard to accept. At the very least, we must accept the possibility of our interconnectedness. As Carol and Philip Zaleski describe in *Prayer: A History*, intercessory prayer opens the possibility that "one individual can take up the burdens of another without increasing the total sum of misery and that one person's merits can be transferred to another's account without decreasing the total sum of grace."

Just as infrequent communication with friends and family results in perfunctory exchanges, occasional prayers or prayers uttered only in moments of anger, fear, or desperation seem less likely to open two-way communication. A regular prayer practice seems more likely to clear a channel to the divine, and many world religions have built this assumption into their structure. Muslims are required to face Mecca to perform *salat*, a fixed prayer ritual, five times a day. Jews pray at least three times daily, and more on high holy days and the Sabbath. Some devout Catholics pray the Angelus, a devotion to Mary, mother of Jesus, three times daily, while many Christian monastic orders follow the ritual of the Divine Office, with prayers at specific times throughout the day and night. This regular, repetitive prayer is devotional in nature, designed to bring the devotee deeply and continuously into the presence of the divine until the self is dissolved.

The practice of centering prayer, as described by Keating, is very close to what Eastern religions refer to as meditation. He suggests using a sacred word, such as Abba, peace, silence, God, or love, as a means of entering a contemplative state. In this state, we learn to accept whatever is happening, including our own thoughts and outer distractions. Keating defines prayer as a way of putting yourself at God's disposal. He reminds us that the important thing is not the prayer itself but the contemplative experience during the time set aside for prayer. With practice, this experience then flows into and enriches our lives.

Contemplation

Contemplation is an enigma; although it requires deep thought and concentration, it is not the same as thinking. In the silence of contemplation, we transcend and transform our mundane thoughts by merging them with something beyond conscious understanding.

All major religious traditions include some form of contemplative practice, but the meaning of the word *contemplation* has evolved over time. It comes from the Latin *templum*, meaning "temple." Its derivative, *contemplari*, "to gaze attentively or observe," implies a religious purpose or object for such attentiveness.

Strictly speaking, a contemplative is someone who has adopted the practice of contemplation as a vocation. We might imagine someone impractical and remote, walled off from the real world in a monastery or convent. Contemplatives have been frowned upon for not taking an active role in life, seeming to avoid rather than grapple with the difficult realities of the world. But deep contemplation opens us to insights that are impossible to discover while we are living in the "real" world. In *Cloister Walk*, Kathleen Norris reminds us that "a contemplative who is being with God, praying with and for the world, is doing something that is invaluable in part because it transcends utility."

In the modern interpretation of the word, contemplation is more about an attitude than a place. We do not need to live in a monastery to adopt an attitude of discernment and consideration that allows us to see the truth. When we contemplate, we become open and attentive to any wisdom, insight, or intuition that we receive. Those who commit time each day to silent prayer, meditation, or contemplation seem to create more opportunity in their lives for this kind of insight.

Contemplation is not always joyful and transcendent. "Pain is one of the sure signs that contemplation is happening," says Parker

Palmer in his book *A Hidden Wholeness*. The American-born mystic Gangaji says in *The Diamond in Your Pocket*, "Opening to whatever is present can be a heartbreaking business." Honest insight into our feelings, families, decisions, and the way we live may not reveal a rosy picture, which could explain why so many of us fear sitting in silence.

The silent periods during singing meditation are relatively brief. Consider them an invitation to follow your heart into the empty spaces. Don't get too hung up on technique. Just be still.

Starting a Group

At the time of this writing, singing meditation is still in its infancy, and ongoing groups meet only in Wisconsin and Florida. If you live elsewhere, you will have to start a group if you want to try it. Some of you may react to this suggestion with an incredulous, "Who? Me?" Maybe you have sung in choirs but never led one. Maybe you don't have a degree in music. Maybe you're not sure your voice is good enough to put yourself in the spotlight. But if you long to taste the sublime joy of singing sacred songs with others, you can use the following guidelines to get started.

Facilitation

Anyone can participate in singing meditation, but that doesn't mean everyone can lead sessions. A good facilitator must have musical ability, self-confidence, patience, humility, and flexibility. If you do not have these characteristics, which are described more fully below, you may need to scout around your church, choir, or community for someone to help you start a group.

The ability to carry a melody line with the voice is critical to successful facilitation. If you have ever been asked by a choir director or small group ensemble to sing a solo, you can be sure your voice is good enough. But even if you haven't, you may still have a perfectly adequate voice to be a facilitator.

Realistically, you must be able to read music to facilitate a group. Learning songs strictly through the oral tradition, while possible, would require a keen memory and a lot of time.

Playing an instrument well enough to pick out the melody line is also a tremendous help. If your voice is loud enough to hold onto the melody, even when other voices wobble, you can get by without playing an instrument proficiently. But reading music well enough to teach yourself a melody is a great asset.

Having a loud voice is also necessary so you can unobtrusively increase your volume, if needed, to correct errors in the group's timing or pitch. Think of your voice as a sheepdog herding the sheep onto the melodic path, nudging the strays along to keep them from leading the flock away from the melody and rhythm. This ability is especially critical when singing rounds. It also helps novice singers tune into the sound of your voice singing the melody line while others sing harmony parts, at least at first. Your voice is the beacon the less-experienced singers follow so they don't have to work too hard to find the notes. If your voice is not loud, use a microphone for a one-hour session. A handheld microphone will do, but a wireless setup is preferable.

If you are thinking about leading singing meditation but aren't sure your voice is good enough, confide in someone whose honesty you respect about your plans. Ask this person to be your listener and sing a short song with only one question: Did I successfully carry the melody? The song should be one your listener knows well—"Happy Birthday" or "Row, Row, Row Your Boat" will do. Sing with no instrumental backup. If your listener says you carried the tune satisfactorily, you are probably good to go. If your listener says you lost the melody, you should reconsider your plan to facilitate, or take voice lessons in preparation.

Another advantage of testing your voice with a listener is that later, if you are having second thoughts about whether it is good enough to lead others, you can remind yourself that your listener has confirmed your ability to carry a simple tune. If you still lack confidence in your voice, ask yourself what *would* give you confidence? Voice lessons? Singing in an established choir? Auditioning and getting a role in community theater? Try to find an achievement you can reflect on and draw strength from when you have self-doubt. Overall, singing as often as possible—to residents of nursing homes, to your grandchildren, or in community chorus—is the best way to improve your singing voice.

A less-than-stellar voice can actually be an asset when facilitating, because it won't discourage others from singing. Ruthie once had the experience of leading a group in a different location than she normally used. She recalls:

> The acoustics of the chapel were perfect, and some unknown combination of atmospheric pressure, humidity, health factors, and emotional state made my voice unusually clear and pure that night. Afterwards, a woman I'd never met approached to congratulate me on my splendid voice, adding that she herself had chosen not to sing at all so as to better enjoy listening to me. I immediately froze inside. This quiet, earnest woman meant to pay me a compliment. Sadly, I recognized that the beauty of my voice had been an impediment to achieving the goal of singing meditation: to create a setting in which each person attending is enveloped into full participation in the group singing.

Zen Buddhists believe we should cultivate a mindset that allows us to act without any attachment to the outcome. If we donate to someone, we do it without expectation of gratitude or the way it will be spent. We focus only on our own choices and actions, leaving behind the emotional attachments that lead to disappointment, anger, pride, or arrogance when the outside world does not view our actions the way we believe they should.

Ideally, you will approach facilitation of singing meditation without ego attachment to the outcome. Think of the session as a feast you are preparing for guests. You don't know how many people will come, whether they will like the food you have prepared, or whether they will bring appropriate additions to the meal. If you spread out your offering assuming and expecting that at least thirty people will arrive, each hungry for the exact dishes you've prepared and bearing the right wine to complement your dessert course, you will spend the entire session in an agony of judgment and assessment. *Does the lady with the glasses like these songs? Only fourteen people came; why not more? Are people enjoying this or just being polite?*

Effective facilitation requires that you remain grounded and centered so that your own ego does not obstruct the flow of energy in the group. Balancing your own energy and preferences with those of the participants requires you to exercise patience and flexibility. You might become so excited about the beautiful sounds that you become greedy for more and more songs, often skimping on the teaching period and/or the silent intervals. Or, you might assume that people will become bored if you spend too much time teaching songs.

That's certainly how Ruthie felt in her first year of leading singing meditation sessions. Then she led a weekend retreat at the Christine Center in Willard, Wisconsin. Here, over an entire weekend, she had enough time to teach the songs slowly. She structured the weekend with learning sessions, teaching some songs on Friday night and some on Saturday morning. On Saturday night, the first real session took place, alternating songs with silence.

Rather than being boring, the longer teaching sessions had actually enhanced the spirituality of the practice. Participants were able to go more deeply into the songs—and the silence—because their brains had moved from early learning activity to the more comfortable repetition of a familiar song. As the spirituality of the session deepened, participants said later that they actually wanted to spend more time in silence.

As a result of this experience, singing meditation now incorporates some more learning mode time, without impatience, into even the shorter one-hour sessions.

The Repertoire

As a facilitator, you must be prepared to teach a variety of appropriate songs. Songs that are short, easy to learn, and easy to sing usually work best in a singing meditation session. At their finest, they should also possess an ineffable attribute we call "spirit," a mysterious quality that swells in our hearts with each repetition, building what Kenneth Bruscia describes in *Defining Music Therapy* as a "bridge between ordinary consciousness of ordinary reality to non-ordinary and expanded consciousness of the infinite." Songs typically used in singing meditation include chants, rounds, songs in harmony, and call and repeat.

Chants, which consist of melody lines without many pitches, are pretty easy to learn. A chant with only one pitch is often referred to as a *drone*. Drones are excellent for participants who are insecure about their singing. They can simply repeat the drone line over and over again, without venturing into learning a melody line.

Chants are intended to help transport us to a transcendent realm. Yoga practices often incorporate ecstatic chant, allowing practitioners to more readily touch and expand their inner mystical state and eventually experience oneness with God. The vibrational patterns produced by chants help to still our overactive minds, calm worries and concerns, and help us to connect with divine love. Mystics describe the mysterious oneness experienced during ecstasy, when the chant and the chanter create a bridge to connect us with the divine, reminding us that we are at once individuals and a part of all creation.

Rounds are excellent for singing meditation. If you don't have enough people to form groups, or the song is new, you can sing rounds in unison to good effect. When you have enough people to split into two or more groups, rounds can provide automatic harmony. The net effect is a richer, more textured song. The Taizé songbooks include several excellent rounds, including "Jubilate Deo," "Magnificat," and "Gloria." Some Jewish rounds that work in the practice are "Hava Nashirah" and "Hineh Mah Tov." Kate Munger's Threshold Choir songbook has over one hundred rounds, most of them appropriate for singing meditation. Hymnals are another good source for rounds.

In a harmony song, a minimum of two different pitches are sung simultaneously. Think of two voices melting together as they croon, "We were sailing along. . . ." The singers usually sing the same words at the same time, but not necessarily. The harmony notes may be already written down by the composer on a piece of paper, or may be freely improvised on the spot.

In call-and-repeat songs, the leader sings out a section of the song, and the group echoes it in response. Some African and kirtan songs use the call-and-repeat format. In singing meditation, we listen not to our own individual voices but to each other's voices. We attune to them. The same is true in call and repeat. Participants don't need to read or memorize lyrics; all intake is through the ears, putting singers into a different mode immediately. It is auditory "music in" and "music out." Both pace and volume can be varied; the more varied the call, the more intensely the group draws together, listening collectively.

Cultural Context

In the practice of singing meditation, we embrace music from many spiritual traditions. We have a responsibility to understand the origins, traditional meaning, and purpose of the music to use it with proper respect. When you consider using a song, the following questions may help you understand more about how to approach its cultural context.

- ∼ What attracts me to the song?
- ∼ What do I know about its background—the traditions, history, or experience of the people from whom it comes? Do I need to explain and acknowledge the history or background of the song?
- ∼ Do the "owners" of this song object to its use by others?

The last question in particular can be difficult to answer. Indeed, it can sometimes be difficult to know who really "owns" a song. A nun at the Saint Hilaire Saint Jean Damascene Orthodox Centre in Uchon, France, seemed surprised when asked how her religious tradition felt about non-Orthodox believers singing Orthodox songs. She offered a three-part response. First, that her community would not find it offensive. Second, that it would be impossible for them to attempt to keep tabs on the entire globe to make sure no one was singing an Orthodox song inappropriately—once the CDs were made and distributed, the community released its control over the music. Finally, she hoped some non-believers would be moved enough by the music to investigate its theology.

Still, the question remains. Knowing one Orthodox nun's opinion about using their music in singing meditation is not the same as getting permission from the community. Given her knowledge of and reverence for Orthodox music, her response is a good indicator, but she could well be in the minority. How many Orthodox nuns or priests would one have to poll before definitively claiming that it is okay to use this music in a spiritual practice? Similarly, reading the liner notes of Ragani's CD, *Best of Both Worlds*, makes it clear that she thinks kirtan is for everyone. But, again, what if hers is a minority opinion?

The best approach is to try to be alert to a specific culture's attitudes about the use of their music and ceremonies by outsiders. If you sense controversies or sensitivities, then steer clear of including that music in your group. Err on the side of caution in this matter, rather than inadvertently disrespecting the sanctity of another person's religious observance.

In addition, we need to exercise caution when adapting a song. On occasion, you may substitute words or delete part of a song that seems too long. Some groups, however, including the Taizé community, state explicitly that they do not permit other arrangements, lyrics, or adaptations of their songs. Taizé songs are not meant to be entertainment, existing independently of the prayers they express. The brothers of Taizé have spent consider-able time, energy, and devotion in creating and refining each song for a particular purpose.

Copyright is another important consideration when selecting a repertoire. There are two ways to avoid copyright infringement: Buy enough copies of the songbooks for each person to use, or don't use printed music. If you sing at a church, as part of a ser-vice, check whether the church has a membership with a copy-right clearance service such as OneLicense (www.onelicense.net). The subscription fees paid by the church may permit you to use a huge variety of music. The church simply reports which songs were used. The church administrator or music director will be fa-miliar with this reporting requirement.

Location

Sessions can be led in churches or in private homes, as long as there is sufficient space, and pets and small children are quiet and well behaved. It is essential that the place be quiet, uncluttered, and a comfortable temperature. Ideally, you should be able to set chairs or cushions in a circle or semicircle to create a communal setting, and to place a small table in the center as a focal point.

A piano or keyboard is a useful addition, as well as sound equipment if your voice is not loud enough to lead without a mi-crophone. If they are not available in the space you plan to use, you will need to carry them to each session.

Lighting is an important element to consider. No one has ever complained during or after a session about seating or room temperature, but occasionally people do want specific changes in lighting. In most spaces, you won't have much control over this element. If you do, try to avoid lights that flicker or that shine directly in anyone's eyes.

If the location requires a rental fee, you will need to charge participants a fee or ask for donations. You might not have enough participants to cover costs, which may complicate the practice of nonattachment to outcome that is necessary to successful facilitation. Consider this matter when choosing your facility.

Publicity

You will have to get the word out about the sessions you're going to lead. You can place posters in public libraries, community centers, coffee shops, or churches. You can also email press releases to local papers or radio stations that offer public service announcements.

Don't hesitate to try unusual outlets or team up with another person or group to draw additional publicity and attract new participants. You might distribute flyers at a musical performance or reach out to another group that holds a regular spiritual practice. A nonprofit in your area might cosponsor a session. You may be surprised at who is attracted to the practice. In Wisconsin, when singing meditation announcements were sent to the music faculty of the local college, somehow the notice reached a professor of religion and philosophy, whose students became frequent attendees.

Simple business cards are wonderful tools for promoting singing meditation. You can easily create and print them at home, with your name, phone number, and email address. Carry them in your wallet so you can easily jot dates and times for the next two sessions on the back of a card for someone who expresses interest.

Remember to bring a sign-up sheet to your sessions to help build an email list. Once you have a list, send a reminder about three days before each event. Always include your own email address or phone number for more information.

Leading a Session

Experience has shown that advance preparation is key to effectively leading singing meditation. When you've done all you can to prepare the songs, the setting, and yourself, it is much easier to approach the session with an attitude of nonattachment to the outcome.

For the average one-hour session, plan to spend at least an hour preparing two song lists. Create one list for the possibility that the entire group will be complete beginners, and another for a group of good singers and/or those experienced with singing meditation.

Occasionally, you may plan a session around a theme such as "winter" or "peace," and select songs related to that topic. More often, the sessions are deliberately eclectic. Lists should include songs that create a variety of moods and energies, not just slow and meditative ones. One of the primary goals of a session is to unplug the busy mind. Switching between various modes of music is a good way to disengage the mind so it is more centered and receptive to the periods of silence between the songs.

In some settings, the organization hosting the event will ask that you select the songs ahead of time, so they can be included in a program, bulletin, or order of service. While not ideal, this request is understandable. Even if this makes you feel boxed in, just graciously do as you've been asked and hope for the best.

Your song list should include six or seven songs that you think will flow well from one to the next, plus some substitutes. Choose some rounds in case the harmony songs prove too musically difficult for the singers that evening. As facilitator, you should feel comfortable singing at least thirty songs, so you'll have sufficient variety to choose from as you respond to your group.

No matter what songs are on your list, always be ready to jettison any of them or to supplement with others from your treasure chest. During the session, you will need to be aware and vigilant on behalf of the group. They trust you to lead them into songs that will soothe, energize, delight, and move them. You must be flexible and respond to signals you pick up from the group. The more songs you know well enough to teach, the more flexible you can be.

You might want to use a few readings during the sessions, such as short poems or quotes, to enhance the effect of the songs. You can distribute quote cards to readers in your group ahead of time and then cue them to read at the appropriate times.

You should warm up your voice before the session, either by softly singing along to the car radio or practicing a song while driving to the session. It also helps to refrain from caffeinated beverages and cold drinks for an hour or two before the session.

Try envisioning the upcoming session. How do you feel while you imagine it? How would you like to feel? What would it take to feel joyful or peaceful or contemplative? You may be able to arrange something in advance—lighting candles, including a certain song, or making a simple announcement that will forestall a problem. If you sense that something might happen that is beyond your control, acknowledge the feeling and remind yourself not to get attached to specific results.

Plan to arrive an hour before the session begins so you'll have time to place chairs in a circle, create the altar, arrange the space, adjust the temperature if possible, light the candles, and put up signs directing people to the correct room within the building. Arriving early leaves you time to be relaxed and welcoming to the participants as they arrive. Once the setting is prepared, you can use the remaining time to attune yourself to the upcoming session and go over your tentative list of songs.

A table in the center of the circle, visible to all participants, makes a good focal point. You can decorate it to visually comple-ment the abundance of musical sources. Scarves, flowers in bloom, evergreen boughs, stones, and seashells work well to create a sa-cred space.

Some groups use angel cards, which are small cards depicting hand-drawn images of angels with single words, such as "peace" or "joy," written on them. The word may be used as an aid to medita-tion or contemplation during the silent periods. These cards are placed face down on the table and participants may draw one or two as they feel moved to do so.

During evening sessions, you may choose to use indirect light-ing supplemented with candlelight. Singing by candlelight alone is ideal but requires everyone to know each song well enough to get by without enough light to read. If you are tempted to use incense or artificial scents, be mindful that members of your group may suffer from allergies or asthma.

Welcome

People come to singing meditation because they have decided they want to sing with others instead of alone, so it is important to recognize the participants and help them feel connected with each other right away. These people bring a great gift—their time, attention, and trust. Use your body language, facial expressions, and words to reassure everyone that you are happy they have made the effort to join you. Smile! Let your welcome show, not your anxiety.

You can safely assume that some participants will be shy, ner-vous, or anxious because this activity is completely new for them. You should explain enough about what is going to happen to put everyone at ease. Even the occasional person who is bubbling with self-confidence will appreciate an explanation. As an alternative, you can distribute an introductory handout explaining the basics of singing meditation, so you don't have to spend time at the beginning of each session repeating that information. For example, you may provide specific information about the length of silent periods and the signal to end silence.

The following sample instructions are intended not as a script to be followed exactly but as a roadmap indicating points of interest that may be touched on at the beginning of a session or in your handout.

What is singing meditation? In singing meditation, we sing a simple line of music over and over until we dissolve into silence. The mindful repetition disconnects our minds from worry and planning and moves us into the present moment. Once the singing has stilled the mind, we hold two to five minutes of undirected silence, then move on to another song.

Everyone is welcome to sing. The quality of the singing voice and the extent of your musical knowledge are not important. What matters is intention and ability to listen to others while singing. No one cares about wrong notes. Ego about one's voice should be surrendered at the door.

Cards. You are invited to select one of the cards displayed on the table. Each card has a word or short phrase on it. You might use this as an anchor word or avenue for reflection during the periods of silence. At the end of the session, quietly return the card to the table. It is entirely up to you whether you wish to share with others the word on your card.

Toning. To warm up the vocal cords, the session may begin with toning, a practice of vocalizing to create long, sustained sounds. Just relax and tone. Don't worry about the pitch you are toning or the quality of your voice.

Learning the songs. The first part of the session may be a learning time, in which the facilitator teaches new songs. During this segment, there are no silent periods between songs. In the actual session, we may sing some songs that have not been taught in the learning time, but everyone will be familiar with at least some of the songs. The facilitator will signal the end of learning mode and the beginning of the song/silence session.

The words. If the words are getting in the way of letting go and getting into the flow of a song, feel free to substitute other sounds such as "la la la" or "oh oh oh." The facilitator will cue the group if pronunciation of the words does matter.

The community around you. Listen to the sound you make, of course, but listen to the sound of the others singing as well.

Taking care of your voice. The best care for the throat is drinking water at room temperature. Do not strain the voice. Never force your singing.

Repetition. Singing the same lines of music multiple times brings us into a state of relaxation and openness to the divine. At first, the repetition of songs may seem strange or boring. One of the best explanations of the benefits of repetitive chant comes from Marlys Brinkman in her Ten-Time Rule of chanting: "The trick to chanting is knowing that the tenth time is the beginning of the work, not the end." See page 85 for the full text of her explanation.

Eyes open or closed. Singing with eyes closed cuts down on distractions, but making eye contact while singing can be very powerful. Experiment with both.

Singing softly. This may happen spontaneously after a song has been sung several times. Singing softly with words or an open vowel sound can be a powerful way to experience the song's vibrations and the vibration of surrounding voices. Letting go of the words lets us abandon one more link to active thinking and deepens connection to the inner core.

Ending the song. Usually, group singing ends with a prearranged signal. In singing meditation, we deliberately do not predetermine the number of repetitions of a song, and there is no signal to stop. We begin to wind down and then collectively dissolve into silence. To be sure none of us need worry or hold back in starting a new repetition, we use this backup plan: If you hear someone else launch into a new repetition, softly hum or sing along in support.

Silence. When a song ends, we sit in silence for two to five minutes. The silence after chanting is as meaningful as the chanting itself. Robert Gass, author of *Chanting*, advises, "Sit in the silence and breathe . . . see if you can feel the vibrations of energy set in movement by the chant reverberating in the space around you and inside your own body. Drink in the subtle presence that often seems to linger in the room." There is no prescribed meditation technique. The goal is to quiet the mind and create a sacred silence. The facilitator will signal the end of the silent period with a predetermined signal, such as a small brass bell or gong.

Feedback and sharing. This one-hour session is not a time for sharing feelings, asking questions, or making comments. Once the instructions are completed, all questions and comments should be held until the session ends.

Teaching the Songs

After the welcome and instructions, you may want to warm up the group with some toning. This is a simple way to ease yourself— and the group—into the practice of singing meditation because there are no words or pronunciation to learn. (See pages 12–13 for specific instructions on toning.) Then announce the first song and explain how you will teach it. Keep the process simple and never assume that everyone will know a particular song.

The Taizé community recommends that practice and learning sessions take place completely separate from the prayer session. This is an excellent idea, however, it is not practical when participants attend on a drop-in basis. Opening the session by teaching four or five songs without silent intervals in between works well. It helps you find out what type of group has assembled and how you can adjust the song list accordingly.

Using a CD to teach songs is not recommended. Experience has shown that, inevitably, a few people in the group become so eager to begin that they just can't listen without singing. Their singing drowns out the CD. Even if they sing correctly, they will do so at their own tempo and fall out of sync with the CD, which can be disconcerting. The others, who aren't singing, hear at least two versions, and perhaps only an auditory blur.

Teaching the melody by playing one note at a time on a piano or small electric keyboard works best. To spice things up, you may feel tempted to play some arpeggios or other arrangements that complement the basic melody line. But these superfluous notes can confuse those who do not read music and negatively affect both the learning process and the aesthetic appeal.

If the song is longer than one line, break it down into smaller blocks to facilitate learning. Play each song or block through once and then sing with the piano once. Ideally, you should play the song through three times on the keyboard. Eager singers always jump in after the first or second time through, so it may be more practical just to go with the flow. If it is a completely new song to the group or is a little tricky, remain seated at the piano the first two times while the group sings a capella and be ready to jump in with piano support if needed. When the group is confident enough without accompaniment, you can join the circle, singing a capella.

You never want participants to feel that singing is too hard for them or that they have failed. Many of us have attended some kind of singing session in which the leader expected people to just join in. For example, a choir director might assume that everyone can read the printed music provided, or the leader of an informal fun group might assume that everyone already knows the song. Maybe a few people can read music or do know the song, and jump right in. But if they don't, they're left sitting there, wishing they could participate but not knowing what's around the next musical bend—a repeat, a chorus, a split into multiple parts. In singing meditation, covering only six songs in an hour session and teaching each song works much better than having a handful of participants sing a dozen songs while the rest of the group feels like failures.

Start with a song that is very easy and completely within your vocal range, one you know so well you could sing it while playing basketball or looking up a phone number. The first song of the first session is not the time to experiment with something new.

John Hakim Bushnell, who leads Dances of Universal Peace in Minnesota, believes that people can find a "group consciousness" more easily if he begins his sessions with music that has a strong rhythm. "Mankind has been drumming and singing for about 100,000 years and we're still hardwired that way," he says. "Using a song with a tribal rhythm lets people tap into the conditioning that's deep within them."

Inexperienced singers often have more difficulty learning songs with harmonies than other, simpler songs. Singing in harmony can be profoundly moving for a group of people, especially if they have never done it before. But since you usually will have assembled a random group of singers, you may need to experiment with introducing harmony. You'll be walking a fine line— you'll want to focus more on meditative and contemplative mode than on learning mode, yet still spend enough time teaching for the novice singers to feel comfortable and included.

One way to teach harmony is to have the sopranos sing the bass line an octave higher and the basses sing the soprano lines an octave lower. After the bass, tenor, alto, and soprano lines have been sung through three or four times individually, people will generally self-select to sing one of those parts, resulting in a harmonious confection—provided that your group has at least one good singer to hold each of the parts. The person with a strong enough voice and good enough ear to hold a harmony part is referred to as the *anchor*.

If you are singing without a piano, and all your singers are novices, do not try to teach harmony lines. Stick to unison, chants, and rounds. Too much emphasis on technical issues and the potential feeling of failure when learning harmony will detract from the spiritual experience.

However, if you have a group with a variety of proficiencies, give them a chance to sing a harmony song at least once during each session to see if any singers are up to the challenge. If you have even one person with strong enough skills to anchor one part while you anchor another, you can teach the melody and one harmony line, even if there are several. Novice singers will be thrilled to take part.

Unfortunately, harmony lines are not learned as easily as the melody line, and even good singers, unless they read music really well, may not find a brief run-through sufficient preparation. Yet practicing a song too much begins to feel like work instead of worship, becoming a negative experience for new singers. Remember, when it feels too much like work, stop teaching harmony songs. Rounds are easier to learn and will still create a harmony effect.

The facilitator needs to listen carefully during all of the songs to make sure no one is struggling. If anyone has difficulty, try one of two strategies: Bring the song to a conclusion as quickly as possible and go into silent meditation, or stop the singing and say, "Wait just a moment; let me teach this song again." Never let people struggle. Singing meditation is about flow and, to the extent possible, that flow should not be interrupted. Songs that cause participants to struggle should be dropped from the repertoire.

The song list should not be carved in stone; choosing a repertoire is an ongoing refining process. During the session, keep up your social antennae and feel the group energy. If it feels draggy instead of contemplative, rejuvenate the group with a livelier song. When facilitating, you won't be in a position to sing a few songs and then, noticing that the group isn't responding as you had hoped, to rifle through a pile of music books, hoping for inspiration. You need to know enough songs to respond to the group energy by substituting alternative songs at a moment's notice. Once you have learned enough songs well and have a group of seasoned singers, you may occasionally want to open up the last half hour or so for requests.

Flowing into Silence

Don't worry about signaling the end of a song. Songs will get louder or softer, faster or slower. When people are really listening to each other and opening their hearts to the music, it will take on a will of its own and eventually end on its own. Only rarely will a person in the group start another iteration of a song after everyone else has stopped. Use the backup plan of singing softly with that person so they will not be embarrassed. Others will probably join in too.

When the song ends, hold silence for two to five minutes. As the facilitator, you need to be mindful not to slip into a trance. The group is depending on you to keep time and signal the end of the silent period. You may also need to slightly vary the length of the silent periods, depending on time of day, outside noise, or group energy.

When the silent period is over, signal the end with a bell or gong. Hold silence for a few more moments before announcing the next song to provide a gentle re-entry for the group.

Closing

Always end with a song rather than a silent period, and make it a joyful one. Song provides a better entrée back into the real world. Unless you are on retreat in a secluded setting, participants leaving a singing meditation session will be going to cars, coping with traffic, and needing to be alert. Ending with a joyful song will put them into a better energy state for making this transition.

Experience has shown that asking participants to observe silence after the session ends does not work well. People want to connect, and if silence is imposed they will start making hand signals to each other until, one by one, they break the silence, either immediately before or just after they reach the door. More important, imposing a "go in silence" rule creates a hardship for newcomers who want to ask a question or join your email list. End in peace. End in joy. Do not end in silence.

The heart of the session has concluded. The last joyful song has been sung. People around the circle are sitting still, basking in the glow of communal delight, reluctant to break the spell. Now is the time to thank everyone for their presence, for the gift of their voices, for the energy they have contributed to the group. Don't be in a rush to tidy up and pack your belongings. Remain available to the group and any individual who may want to connect with you.

Facilitators should be flexible, open to the spirit, and attentive to all participants. Leading singing meditation is a joyful experience. Experiment with joy!

Songs

Fill Your Cup
(The Fish in the Water's Not Thirsty)

Fill   your cup,   drink   it up!

Perc.

Ya   Al - lah, Al - lah!_____ Fill your cup,

drink   it up!   Ya Al - lah, Al - lah!

Words and music © 2002, 2009 Allaudin Ottinger
Words based on a poem by Kabir

Fill Your Cup–2

Ram,   ram,   ram,   ram,   ram,   ram,

ram,   ram,   ram,   ram,   ram,   ram!   The

fish   in   the   wa - ter's   not   thir - sty!

(Ram is pronounced "rahm.")

Dhanyavad

Dhan-ya-vad,   Dhan-ya-vad,   Dhan-ya-vad   a - nan-da.

Dhan-ya-vad, ___   Dhan-ya-vad,   Dhan-ya-vad   a - nan - da.

Words and music © 1999 Henry Marshall

May There Be Peace

Words and music © 2005 Nickomo Clarke

Mother I Feel You

1. Moth - er I feel___ you___ un - der my feet,
2. Moth - er I hear you in the riv - er song
3. Fa - ther I see you when the ea - gle flies

Moth-er I___ hear___ your___ heart___ beat.___
E - ter - nal wa - ters flow-ing on and on.___
Light of the Spir - it, gon - na take us high - er.

He - ya he - ya he - ya ya he - ya he - ya ho

He - ya he - ya he - ya he - ya he - ya ho.___

Words and music © 1996 Windsong Dianne Martin

Namaste

Na - ma - ste

Na - ma - ste

Na - ma - ste

Na - ma - ste

Na - ma - ste

Na - ma - ste

Na - ma - ste

Na - ma - ste

Words and music © 2002 Nickomo Clarke

Nigun No. 10

Nigunim traditionally have no lyrics, using only sounds or syllables. Feel free to develop other patterns.

Traditional Jewish

Radhe Govinda Bolo

Ra - dhe   Ra - dhe   Ra - dhe   Go - vin - da bo - lo,

Ra - dhe   Ra - dhe   Ra - dhe   Go - vin - da bo - lo

Go - vin - da, Go - vin - da,   Go - vin - da,   Ra - dhe

Go - vin - da, Go - vin - da,   Go - vin - da,   Ra - dhe

bol, Ra-dhe   bol, Ra-dhe bol, Ra-dhe   bol,   Ra-dhe Ra-dhe Ra-dhe

bol,   Ra-dhe bol,   Ra-dhe bol,   Ra-dhe bol.

Traditional Hindu

Use Me
(A Channel for Light)

Use me,   use me,   use me,   use me.

Let   me   be   a   chan - nel   for   light,   a

chan - nel   for   grace,   a   chan - nel   for   peace.

* indicates entrance points for singing as a round, if
desired. Another option is to have one group repeat the
first line while the second group sings lines 2 and 3.

Cherish This Hour

* indicates entrance points for singing as a round.

Joy

Let joy fill your heart, may peace be your goal.

May joy, peace and love make us whole.___

* Indicates entrances of other voices for round.

* indicates entrance points for singing as a round.

Chanting: The Ten-Time Rule

Marlys Brinkman, choir director at Boulder Valley Unitarian Universalist Fellowship in Lafayette, Colorado, distributes the following handout to people when they first try chanting. It explains the brain's typical reaction to the repetitiveness of chant.

When chanting, it is important not to stop too soon. The benefits of chanting are surprisingly satisfying if you give yourself time to experience the deepening aspects of the chant.

Often a person will go through a rainbow of emotions when first learning to chant. It is completely normal to feel a bit anxious at first, then perhaps bored, even annoyed during part of the chanting. Thoughts such as, "Why are we doing this so long? When are we going to be done? What's the matter with everyone? This is boring!" come to mind and distract us for a moment or two as we experience negative feelings. Actually, this is a normal phase of chanting, a part of the growing into chanting, and, if you just keep going with a sense of trust in the work, you come out of that semidarkness into a sense of light and connection. Some call it a place of wonder, or of deep peace.

Here's an example of the phases:

- 1st time—The chant is new; you are concentrating on singing it right.

~ 2nd time—You do it a bit more "correctly," and make only a few mistakes.

~ 3rd time—You sing it right all the way through; you feel a sense of accomplishment.

~ 4th time—You now can sing it right without much effort. You begin to think, *Now what?*

~ 5th time—You feel a bit of annoyance. *Hey, I've got this down. We can stop now.*

~ 6th time—You are bored, tired of it, your mind is objecting to this waste of time. *This is stupid.*

(Sometimes you get stuck in the 6th time, but, if you stay with it, your mind will go to the 7th time after a few more reps)

~ 7th time—You give up, mentally throw your hands up, and think, *Oh well, we're probably going to go on forever, so I guess I'll just relax.*

~ 8th time—You feel that relaxation, and sort of enjoy it.

~ 9th time—As you continue to enjoy the relaxation, you begin to feel something deeper now. Your mind is quiet, taking a mini-vacation, while you are doing this boring (to its way of thinking) activity.

~ 10th time—You continue to relax, feel the ebb and flow of the chant. Without noticing it, you are opening to a larger part of yourself, and the chanting is the doorway. A whole new way of experiencing is just beyond the threshold of this door. You feel more relaxed and more at peace, and you feel healing energy flowing within you as you sing this simple chant. You walk through this doorway and begin.

The trick to chanting is knowing that the tenth time is the *beginning* of the work, not the end.

Glossary

a cappella Vocal music sung without instrumental accompaniment. From the Italian, meaning "in the chapel."

apophatic Theology based on the assumption that God is unknowable and therefore cannot be described in human language or depicted by human images. Also referred to as *via negativa*, the negative way, i.e., God is what cannot be described or known.

appropriation A term used to signify the act of borrowing or using practices from other cultures or traditions.

bhajan Hindu devotional song (kirtan) expressing love for the divine.

call and repeat A musical form in which a leader or soloist sings or plays a section of music, and a group or chorus echoes it in response.

call and response A musical form in which a leader or soloist sings or plays the melody and a group or chorus sings another musical phrase as a reaction to or commentary on the first.

cataphatic Theology based on the belief that God, incarnate as Jesus Christ, can be described and approached through human thoughts and images. Also referred to as *via positiva*, the positive way, i.e., humans can know and describe God.

centering prayer A contemporary contemplative prayer practice developed by Thomas Keating and others, which uses a sacred word as a means of entering the contemplative state.

chant Considered the most ancient form of choral music, it has a short, simple melody and is often used to recite sacred texts.

contemplative prayer A Christian prayer practice that endeavors to fully open the mind and heart to the presence of the divine.

Dances of Universal Peace A spiritual practice that unites sacred movement, song, and story from many world traditions. Its origins are Sufi, but today it incorporates music and text from many religions and traditions.

drone A continuous pitch (monotone) usually played in the bass and sustained or persistently repeated throughout a piece of music.

Gregorian chant A collection of Roman Catholic liturgical chants whose origins have been lost. They were used to accompany the Catholic Mass and other rituals as early as the sixth century.

harmony Music in which more than one pitch or note is sung or chanted at the same time by two or more singers. This combination is referred to as *chords*. Harmony is generally pleasing to the ear.

kirtan The devotional practice of chanting sacred hymns (from Sanskrit "to repeat"). The term refers both to individual chants and songs, and to the act of participating in the practice. Kirtan is not specific to one religious tradition.

mantra A sacred syllable, sound, or word frequently used during meditation, ritual, or chant in many spiritual traditions. The meaning or use of the mantra varies according to tradition; it may contain or mirror the essence or name of the divine, invoke cosmic vibrations, contain magical power, or protect the mind from incorrect perceptions and ideas.

melody The tune or string of notes that forms a musical composition. The melody is the most important, or dominant, line of the music.

misappropriation Name sometimes applied to circumstances in which the practices or traditions of a particular culture are misused, exploited, or misinterpreted by those from a different culture.

nigun A sacred Jewish song that is part of a body of music referred to collectively as *nigunim*. Most nigunim are wordless and typically sung a capella.

pitch The relative highness or lowness of a tone. Pitch is determined by a sound's frequency of vibration; the greater the frequency, the higher the pitch.

qawwali A form of sacred Islamic vocal music, originating in Pakistan and India.

raga In Hindu music, a melody that expresses a certain theme or religious feeling, based on a set pattern of tones, progressions, and rhythms.

round A musical composition for two or more voices in which each voice repeats exactly the same melody, beginning at different times. "Row, Row, Row Your Boat" is perhaps the most well-known round in the United States.

Sacred Harp singing A form of sacred choral music that originated in New England in the eighteenth century. The original Sacred Harp songbook used musical notation printed in special shapes (so-called shape notes) that helped the singer to identify them.

Sanskrit The classic literary language of India, traditionally used for religious and sacred writing.

shape note singing Synonymous with Sacred Harp singing.

singing meditation A spiritual practice that alternates singing a variety of simple spiritual songs with periods of silence.

Taizé A contemplative Christian worship that originated at the Taizé community in the small village of Taizé, located in the Burgundy region of France.

tala In Indian classical music, a pattern that determines the rhythmical structure of a composition.

toning The practice of vocalizing to create long, sustained sounds, usually open vowel sounds or single syllables without meaning.

Resources

Books

St. Augustine. *Confessions*. R.S. Pine-Coffin, trans. Harmondsworth: Penguin, 1961.

Berglund, Brad. *Reinventing Sunday: Breakthrough Ideas for Transforming Worship*. Valley Forge, PA: Judson Press, 2001.

Bruscia, Kenneth E. *Defining Music Therapy*. Gilsum, NH: Barcelona Publishers, 1998.

Campbell, Don. *The Healing Powers of Tone and Chant*. Wheaton, IL: Quest Books, 1994.

_____. *The Mozart Effect: Tapping the Power of Music to Heal the Body, Strengthen the Mind and Unlock the Creative Spirit*. New York: HarperCollins, 2001.

Cooper, David A. *Silence, Simplicity and Solitude: A Guide for Spiritual Retreat*. New York: Crown Publishing, 1992.

Gangaji. *The Diamond in Your Pocket*. Boulder, CO: Sounds True, 2005.

Gardner-Gordon, Joy. *The Healing Voice: Traditional and Contemporary Toning, Chanting and Singing*. Freedom, CA: The Crossing Press, 1993.

Gass, Robert. *Chanting: Discovering Spirit in Sound*. New York: Broadway Books, 1999.

Gaynor, Mitchell L. *The Healing Power of Sound: Recovery from Life-Threatening Illness Using Sound, Voice, and Music*. Boston: Shambhala Publications, 2002.

Jensen, Eric. *Music with the Brain in Mind*. Thousand Oaks, CA: Corwin Press, 2000.

Keating, Thomas. *Open Mind, Open Heart*. New York: Continuum, 2006.

Keyes, Laurel Elizabeth. *Toning: The Creative Power of the Voice*. Marina del Rey, CA: deVorss, 1973.

Levitin, Daniel J. *This Is Your Brain on Music*. New York: Penguin Group, 2007.

Lyon, David. *Postmodernity*. Minneapolis: University of Minnesota Press, 1999.

Marini, Stephen A. *Sacred Song in America: Religion, Music, and Public Culture*. Chicago: University of Illinois Press, 2003.

Palmer, Parker J. *A Hidden Wholeness: The Journey Toward an Undivided Life*. San Francisco: Jossey-Bass, 2004.

Rasor, Paul. *Faith Without Certainty*. Boston: Skinner House Books, 2005.

Swami Sivananda. *Mantras: Words of Power*. Kootenay, British Columbia: Timeless Books, 2005.

Wikstrom, Erik Walker. *Simply Pray: Modern Spiritual Practice to Deepen Your Life*. Boston: Skinner House Books, 2005.

Norris, Kathleen. *The Cloister Walk*. New York: Riverhead Books, 1996.

Zaleski, Carol, and Philip, Zaleski. *Prayer: A History*. Boston: Houghton Mifflin, 2005.

Songbooks

Boyer, Horace Clarence, ed. *Lift Every Voice and Sing II: The African American Hymnal.* New York: Church Publishing Incorporated, 1993.

Grigolia, Mary. *Voices from the Path,* self-published, available from: www.marygrigolia.com.

_____. *Commitment to a Vision,* vol. 2, self-published, available from: www.marygrigolia.com.

Libana. *A Circle Is Cast: Rounds, Chants and Songs for Celebration and Ritual.* Cambridge, MA: 1986, self-published.

_____. *Night Passage, Invocations for the Journey.* Cambridge, MA: 2000, self-published.

Nickomo/The Harmonic Temple. *Here Right Now: Harmonies of the Spirit,* self-published, available from: www.nickomoandrasullah.com.

_____. *Ateh Malkuth.* self-published, available from: www.nickomoandrasullah.com.

Swetina, Barbara, editor. *Songs of Heaven and Earth.* Findhorn, Scotland: Findhorn Foundation, 2003, available from: www.sacredsongs.net.

_____. *When Two or More Are Gathered...: Sing-Along Songs for the Heart and Soul.* Findhorn, Scotland: Findhorn Foundation, 2003, available from: www.sacredsongs.net.

Taizé Community. *Chants de Taizé.* Taizé, France: Ateliers et Presses de Taizé, 2008.

_____. *Songs and Prayers from Taizé.* Taizé, France: Ateliers et Presses de Taizé, 1991.

Unitarian Universalist Association. *Singing the Journey.* Boston: UUA, 2006.

_____. *Singing the Living Tradition.* Boston: UUA, 1993.

Women with Wings. *Hand in Hand and Heart to Heart: Original Chants and Songs of Affirmation and Empowerment*. Bolivar, MO: Quiet Waters Publications, 2005.

Recorded Music

Findhorn Foundation Community Singers. *Songs of Heaven and Earth, Songs of Celebration from Around the World*. Findhorn Foundation, 2001.

_____. *When Two or More Are Gathered: Sing-Along Songs for Heart and Soul*. Findhorn Foundation, 2000.

Gass, Robert. *Chant: Spirit in Sound, the Best of World Chant*. Spring Hill Music, 1999.

Gass, Robert/On Wings of Song. *Ancient Mother*. Spring Hill Music, 1993.

_____. *Medicine Wheel*. Spring Hill Music, 1992.

_____. *Songs of Healing*. Spring Hill Music, 1992.

Holmes Brothers. *Jubilation*. Real World Records, 1992.

Kaplan, Richard. *Life of the Worlds, Journeys in Jewish Sacred Music*. Five Souls Music, 2003.

KIVA. *Mother Wisdom: Original and Traditional Chants*. Kiva, 1994.

Libana. *A Circle Is Cast*. 2000.

_____. *Night Passage*. 1986.

Maniko. *House of the Beloved: Ecstatic Groove and Songs of Divine Conspiracy*. Isness Records, 2003.

Nickomo/The Harmonic Temple. *Ateb Malkuth: Four-part Chants and Canons to Texts from Various Spiritual Traditions*. 1998.

_____. *Here Right Now*. 2002, available from: www.nickomoandrasullah.com.

_____. *Singing with the Angels*. 2005, available from: www.nicko-moandrasullah.com.

Ottinger, Allaudin. *In the Everywhere and Always*. Dances of Universal Peace Music, 2005.

Ragani. *Best of Both Worlds*. Sacred kirtan music. Prosperity Matters, 2003. www.raganiworld.com.

Shades of Praise. *God Is Still Doing Great Things*. Shades of Praise: the New Orleans Interracial Gospel Choir, 2004.

Summerwood, Marie. *She Walks With Snakes, Women's Sacred Chants*. 1998.

Taizé. *Alleluia*. Ateliers et Presses de Taizé, 1988.

_____. *Jubilate*. Ateliers et Presses de Taizé, 1991.

_____. *Laudate Omnes Gentes*. Ateliers et Presses de Taizé, 2003.

_____. *Ubi Caritas*. Ateliers et Presses de Taizé, 1996.

_____. *Wait for the Lord*. GIA Productions, 1987.

Threshold Choir, Kate Munger. *Tenderly Rain*. 2006, available from: Kate Munger, Box 173, Inverness, CA 94937, www.thresholdchoir.org.

_____. *Listening at the Threshold*. 2004, available from: Kate Munger, Box 173, Inverness, CA 94937, www.thresholdchoir.org.

Van Dyke, Deborah. *Traveling the Sacred Sound Current: Divine Chants and Sacred Tones for Healing and Meditation*. Sound Current Music, 2001.

Velez, Glen. *Rhythms of the Chakras: Drumming for the Body's Energy Centers*. Sounds True, 1998.

Wolfsong, Leah. *Songs of the Circle*. Roots Down Music, 2000.

Websites

American Music Therapy Association, www.musictherapy.org

Blue Mountain Meditation—Eight Point Program, www.easwaran.org

Dances of Universal Peace, www.dancesofuniversalpeace.org

Dave Stringer, Kirtan, www.davestringer.com

Findhorn Foundation, www.findhorn.org

Findhorn Music Books, www.sacredsongs.net

Nickomo and Harmonic Temple, www.nickomoandrasullah.com

OneLicense Copyright Reprints for Congregational Song (Copyright permissions), www.onelicense.net

Singing Meditation, www.singingmeditation.com

Shades of Praise Gospel Choir, www.shadesofpraise.org

Taizé Community, www.taize.fr/en

Acknowledgments

The authors would like to thank Keith Arnold, Marlys Brinkman, David Burrows, John Hakim Bushnell, Stephen Brown, Lyn Dean, Bob Harper, Tim and Karen Hirsch, Tess Larson, Hallie Moore, Perry Pike, Jan Prince, Margee Stienecker, Barb Scherer, Patty Scott, Katy Taylor, Chris Walton, and Andrew Wilke for their help and kindness in preparing this book.

We deeply appreciate the musical contributions, talent, and enthusiasm of our Musical Consultant, Helen Gierke.

A special thank you to Kenn Amdahl for his insightful suggestions to early versions of this book.

We also thank our husbands, Mark Rosauer and Matt Alspaugh, for their unfailing support and patience.